MW01716759

The Sermon on the Mount
A Study Guide

The Sermon on the Mount
A Study Guide

By
T. C. Smith

Smyth & Helwys

ISBN 1–880837–05–6

The Sermon on the Mount.
A Study Guide

Copyright © 1992
Smyth & Helwys Publishing, Inc.

All rights reserved.
Printed in the United States of America.

Biblical quotations, unless otherwise noted,
are from the Revised Standard Version of the Bible,
copyright 1946, 1952, © 1971, 1973
by the Division of Christian Education of the National
Council of Churches of Christ in the U.S.A.,
and are used by permission.

The paper used in this publication
exceeds the minimum requirements of
American National Standard for Information Sciences-
Permanence of Paper for Printed Library Materials

Smyth & Helwys Publishing, Inc.
P. O. Box 72
Greenville, South Carolina 29602

CONTENTS

**This book is dedicated
to all those who uphold truth and freedom
and refuse to be intimidated
by the witch hunting forces that oppose them.**

PREFACE

While I was engaged in a graduate program at New College, University of Edinburgh, Scotland, it was my privilege, during the winter term of 1946, to hear lectures on the Sermon on the Mount given by Professor William Manson, my adviser in graduate studies. His ability to see and understand clearly the inner nature of the teachings of Jesus overwhelmed me. His penetrating insights have made a lasting impression on my life. It is very unfortunate that his lectures were never incorporated in a book.

In 1955-56 while on sabbatical leave from The Southern Baptist Theological Seminary, Louisville, Kentucky, I went to Hebrew Union College, Cincinnati, Ohio to study rabbinic literature for the purpose of understanding Judaism of the first century A.D. Professors Guttmann, Sandmel, and Rivkin were very influential in aiding me to explore in depth the teachings of Pharisaism and at the same time to become aware of a Jewish perception of the teachings of Jesus. Their scholarly contributions have guided me beyond measure in my interpretations of the teachings of Jesus in the Sermon on the Mount.

For twelve years (1946-58) I attempted to squeeze in enough time to concentrate on the study of the Sermon on the Mount. In the fall of 1958 this opportunity came when I was appointed to the faculty of the Divinity School, University of Chicago, as Visiting Professor and Research Scholar. Dr. Walter Harrelson, Dean of the Divinity School, granted me the privilege of plying my energies toward a fuller understanding of the Sermon on the Mount.

Though I have had a consuming interest in the Sermon on the Mount and have spent many additional hours in the study of it since 1958, the opportune time did not arise for the preparation of a manuscript to be published until now. Since the January Bible Study for the Southern Baptist Convention in 1993 is on the Sermon on the Mount, I was prompted to have this book published as an alternative volume for study among Southern Baptists. The treatment of this subject has arisen out of a desire to share my reflections with others as clearly and as concisely as possible. This book is written for those who are partners in a commitment to translate the teachings of Jesus into daily living.

I wish to acknowledge my indebtedness to two of the distaff members of my family. My daughter-in-law, Diane Smith, graciously volunteered to type my manuscript, and my wife, Ellen Bernice, aided me in smoothing out some of the obscure portions when she was proofreading the material.

T. C. Smith
Simpsonville
South Carolina

INTRODUCTION

The Influence of the Sermon on the Mount

From the time that Jesus delivered the Sermon on the Mount until the present day, the message contained in it has had a profound influence not only upon Christendom but the pagan world as well. It has been the impetus for social reform, passive resistance, respect for women's rights, love for one's enemies, acceptance of persecution, forgiving others, genuineness in giving and prayer, seeking spiritual values above material values, upholding the sanctity of human life, and recognizing the sacredness of marriage.

John Wesley, who, along with his brother Charles and others, laid the foundations for Methodism, preached thirteen sermons from the Sermon on the Mount.[1] Some of these homilies were rather lengthy by modern standards. Perhaps the interest of modern day Methodists in social action issues from the special emphasis that Wesley gave to the Sermon on the Mount. Leo Tolstoy, the Russian author of *War and Peace*, *Anna Karenina*, and later in his life many religious books, believed that the Sermon on the Mount, literally interpreted, was the supreme law of the Christian life. He was also famous for stressing especially the precept "resist not evil." Mahatma Gandhi of India, though not directly influenced by the Sermon on the Mount, was swayed by the writings of Tolstoy that upheld passive resistance, and by means of the power of passive resistance he was able to bring to an end the Hindu caste discrimination against the "untouchables" and to spark the movement that led to the liberation of India from British dominance. Martin Luther King, Jr., influenced by the Sermon on the Mount and the success of Gandhi, by means of passive resistance closed the book on segregation in the South and succeeded in effecting a modicum of liberty and justice for all.

Interpretations of the Sermon on the Mount

While the Sermon on the Mount has made an indelible impression upon the Christian community and society at large which may or may not be related to Christian commitment, many ways and means of interpreting its message have been transmitted to us. (1) The Roman Catholic interpretation makes a distinction between *praecepta* or *lex* (percepts or law) and *concilia* (counsels). This view distinguishes between the disciples and the crowds who heard the sermon. The obedience of the disciples to the precepts and the counsels is essential for perfection, and the obedience of the crowds to the precepts is necessary for salvation. Only those who are willing to take the vows of poverty and chastity can achieve perfection. The Roman Catholic interpretation sets up a double standard, thus the radical nature of the sermon is reserved for the few, and the many can be excused for not obeying the Sermon on the Mount.

(2) Martin Luther probably derived his doctrine of two realms primarily from the Sermon on the Mount. Rather than divide the church into two groups—one called upon to obey the precepts only and the other under obligation to obey the precepts and the counsels—he constructed a double standard of a different sort. Luther chose to divide humanity into two realms: the spiritual and the secular. The Christian lives in both

spheres. According to this doctrine God's rule seems to be confined to the invisible and the unpolitical sphere of a person or to the private life of thoughts and attitudes of Christians. In the secular world a Christian does not have the freedom to live by the principles set forth in the Sermon on the Mount. Yet there is nothing found in the sermon that would give rise to a separation within the Christian's life that limits obedience to private spiritual life and thought. It could very well be that this doctrine of two realms is partly responsible for the inaction of the majority of Lutherans in Germany when Hitler and the Nazis were leading Germany down the path to disaster.

(3) Leo Tolstoy's interpretation eliminates the double standard in the church and in the life of the individual. According to him, to be a Christian means to obey Christ's commandments with one's total personality both in individual living and society and in the church and political life. He recognized no other law than the will of God proclaimed in the sermon. Tolstoy believed that Christian faith was total obedience, or it could not be classified as faith. After closely examining Tolstoy's exposition of the Sermon on the Mount, Bornkamm concluded, "that in it all Jesus' commandments are reduced to a purely negative statement: 'thou shalt not resist evil'."[2] Bornkamm was also of the opinion that Tolstoy was not concerned with the positive commandment of love and relationship between God and people and people with people, but was more interested in the teachings of Jesus in the Sermon on the Mount as "a kind of technique of passivity which is to lead man to a rational experience."[3]

(4) Rudolf Bultmann and Martin Dibelius, influenced by Wilhelm Herrmann, argued that the teachings of the sermon are not laws but prescriptions. The teachings liberate us from the law and a legalistic interpretation of the Christian faith. The

sermon sets forth the absolute will of God. It is only as a person submits to God's rule by a change of attitude, thought, and disposition that God's will is understood, and "whoever has his will set upon God's reign also wills to fulfill the commandment of love."[4] It is then and only then that the person no longer looks upon the commandment of love as an annoying duty but as a privilege to follow God's will. The key to the interpretation of Bultmann and Dibelius is Matthew 7:16-19.

(5) Albert Schweitzer, as well as Johannes Weiss, explained that the teachings of Jesus had to be understood against the backdrop of intertestatmental Jewish apocalypticism and highly charged eschatological expectations. They thought that Jesus and the first generation of Christians expected an apocalyptic cosmic catastrophe and believed that the establishment of God's kingdom was imminent. The interim period between their preaching and the kingdom's coming was believed to be very short. Therefore, the message of the sermon was meant to be followed only during the short interim period and not intended as ethical principles for centuries to come. Thus for Schweitzer, the Sermon on the Mount was an "interim ethic," and since the catastrophic end-time did not come, Christian ethics should not be constructed from the teachings of the Sermon on the Mount but rather based on the principle of reverence for life. Schweitzer and Weiss were both in error in attributing to the sermon an apocalyptic slant because it never had it.

(6) Modern day dispensationalism, introduced to American fundementalism in 1909 by C.I. Scofield in his *Scofield Reference Bible*, divided the Bible into seven periods of time. There were seven such dispensations, five in the Old Testament and two in the New Testament. The two dispensations in the New Testament are Grace and Kingdom. According to Scofield

the Christian today lives in the dispensation of Grace. It is only in the stage of Kingdom that the teachings of Jesus in the Sermon on the Mount, as well as other teachings of Jesus, are to be applied in an absolute manner. Strangely enough, this view has captured the attention of many evangelical fundamentalists in our country. Yet the whole system concocted by Scofield is based on flimsy evidence and unrestrained fanciful imagination.

(7) Karl Barth, Dietrich Bonhöffer, and Eduard Thurneysen began their interpretation of the Sermon on the Mount at the place where other interpreters ceased. They all assumed that the message of Jesus given in Matthew 5-7 could not be separated from the rest of Matthew's Gospel, especially the passion narrative. Thurneysen appropriately said, "the post Easter congregation in whose midst the sayings of the Sermon on the Mount were written, read, and heard . . . had always heard in them God's Christ, risen from the dead and exalted, living in the spirit and present among them."[5]

Indeed, it is only as we experience him who is the proclaimed one that we fully comprehend the message of him who proclaimed. Harvey K. McArthur lists twelve interpretations of the Sermon on the Mount, however, it is quite noticeable that some of these proposals spill over into views accepted by individuals or groups in the seven clasifications which I have given.[6]

Understanding Jesus' Teachings in the Sermon on the Mount

Jesus used various methods of teaching. Because the vast majority of his listeners could not grasp truth in a straight forward manner and because of their spiritual ineptitude as Isaiah had described it hundreds of years before (Isa 6:9ff.), Jesus resorted to the parabolic method. In addition to parables he employed the "Question and Answer" format. We might also say that the miracles he performed contained teaching. This is more apparent in John's Gospel that in the Synoptics. In John's Gospel the wonder works are "signs" which reveal spiritual meanings beyond the bare-faced miracle. In the Sermon on the Mount we confront a type of teaching that is straight forward. While the sermon ends with a parable of the two builders, and there are some metaphors which some would categorize as parables, most of the material is more in the form of direct teaching.

At the outset in a study of the Sermon on the Mount there are several questions that have to be asked. What is the setting of the sermon? Who are the ones who make up the audience? How is the sermon related to the account in Luke's Gospel? Should we consider the possibility that Matthew has added material which Jesus taught on other occasions? What are the sources for both Matthew and Luke?

The Setting for the Sermon

What is the setting for the Sermon on the Mount? We shall not attempt to discuss the setting in Jewish messianic expectations, in contemporary Judaism, in the early Church, or in the ministry of Jesus as W.D. Davis has so skillfully delineated.[7] My only interest just here is to consider the site where Jesus delivered the sermon. According to Matthew great crowds followed Jesus from Galilee, the Decapolis, Jerusalem, Judea, and from beyond the river Jordan, and when he saw the crowds, he went up on the mountain (hill) and taught his disciples (4:25-5:1). Luke has Jesus going to a mountain to pray. He continued in prayer all night. The next day he called his disciples and chose twelve, whom he called apostles. After the selection of the twelve he came down with his disciples and stood on a level place. At this level place a large crowd of disciples and a multitude of people from Judea, Jerusalem, Tyre, and Sidon came to hear him and to be healed.

There is a difference between Matthew and Luke concerning the site of the sermon. In Matthew Jesus spoke while seated on a mountain, but in Luke Jesus stood on a level place. Did Matthew have a Moses motif in mind by his selection? Did he intend to convey the notion that Jesus was a new Moses giving a new law from a new mountain? Is it likely that the source for both Matthew and Luke omitted any reference to a location? Scholars generally accept the idea that Matthew and Luke obtained these teachings from a common source called "Q," and that this source contained the sayings of Jesus without any suggestion as to a setting.

The Audience for the Sermon

Another question has to do with the audience. We would assume from Matthew 5:1 that Jesus delivered these teachings to his disciples. Whether these disciples were only the twelve or a larger group, he does not say. At the end of the sermon, however, it is clearly evident that the crowds and not just his disciples were astonished at his teaching. Luke on the other hand says that a crowd of disciples and a multitude of people from various areas came to him on a level place, but he lifted up his eyes on his disciples and began the sermon (6:17-20). Though Luke may indicate that the sermon was directed toward his disciples, he does not exclude the crowds of people who were present.

The Sermon in Matthew and Luke

How is the sermon related to the account in Luke's Gospel? The sermon in Matthew's Gospel is four times as long as the one in Luke. Matthew has 107 verses while Luke has only 29 1/2 verses. They both begin with what we commonly call the Beatitudes and end with the parable of the two builders. In addition to the 29 1/2 verses in Chapter 6 of Luke, there are 34 more verses that are parallel to Matthew, but they are scattered throughout the Gospel of Luke (chs. 11, 12, 13, 16). We notice that there are 45 verses in Matthew's sermon which have no parallels in Luke. In Matthew there are eight (or nine) beatitudes (the eighth and ninth are both related to persecution). Luke has four beatitudes, and these are followed by four woes. Matthew omits the woes, but later in his Gospel he includes seven woes (ch. 23). It is also noticeable that Matthew in the beatitudes uses the third personal pronoun plural in addressing the audience with the exception of verse 11 where he inserts the second person plural. On the other hand Luke uses the second person plural both in the beatitudes and the woes.

Are we to suppose that Jesus gave the full Sermon on the Mount on one particular occasion as Matthew indicates? It is quite possible because it is much shorter than sermons we hear today. Yet when we consider certain matters, it does not appear that Jesus gave all the teachings on one day. (1) The similarities, differences, and omissions as they relate to both Luke and Matthew lead us to conclude that each has collected teachings that were not originally connected. (2) In the other Gospels Jesus' discourses are not lengthy but rather short. (3) The five topical groupings found in Matthew's Gospel would suggest that the author has collected materials given on other occasions by Jesus, but he perceived that they were appropriately related to the categories he had selected.

It is generally accepted among New Testament scholars that Matthew used three sources for his Gospel. The Gospel of Mark was written before Matthew, and the author followed the general outline presented by Mark. In addition to Mark we detect material in both Matthew and Luke which is not found in Mark. While we do not possess the document that Matthew and Luke used, it is commonly referred to as "Q," a written source which would have included sayings of Jesus. As long as Matthew and Luke have parallel information we can conclude that they are following Q. In the event that Matthew includes material not present in Mark and absent from Luke, we assume that Luke decided to omit the teachings. In like fashion when Luke inserts teachings not found in Matthew, we assume that Matthew and Luke had their own peculiar sources in addition to Q and Mark.

Since Luke has 63 1/2 verses of the content of the Sermon on the Mount, though admittedly 34 of these verses are scattered throughout the Gospel, what are we to say about the possibility of the relationships of these two Gospels to their source Q? Shall we say that Luke followed Q faithfully and did not scatter these teachings? Or shall we say that Matthew was faithful to Q and gave the teachings in the Q order? To select either view is a matter of pure conjecture. Since Matthew's sermon has eight parallels to Mark's Gospel which are part of the 45 verses found in Matthew and not in Luke, it is likely that the remaining 37 verses came from a source other than Q.

The author of Matthew's Gospel from the beginning of chapter 3 to the end of chapter 4 followed the events in Mark's Gospel very closely until verse 21 of chapter 1. At this juncture Jesus and his disciples came to Capernaum, and on the sabbath he taught the people in the synagogue. Those who listened were amazed at his teaching because he taught with the authority of an ordained rabbi and not as an unordained scribe.[8] Later in the synagogue service Jesus exorcised an unclean spirit from a man. Again astonishment is registered by the audience so much so that they said, "What is this thing? A new teaching! With authority he commands even the unclean spirits, and they obey him" (Mark 1:27). According to the Pharisees only those teachers who had received ordination (*semikha*) could heal and teach with authority (*reshuth*). Thus what the rabbis claimed for themselves alone—the ability to introduce novel doctrines and perform the function of a physician by the authority given to them in ordination—Jesus was able to do without having been duly ordained.

Since Matthew ends his Sermon on the Mount with what is narrated in Mark 1:22, it seems reasonable to assume that when he came across the astonishment of the crowds in Mark relative to Jesus' authority to give novel teachings, he decided to insert a collection of Jesus' teachings to demonstrate the newness of them. At the same time he probably was eager to show that Jesus' authority bypassed the tradition of derived authority of the rabbis and was more akin to that of Moses who received his authority directly from God.

Notes

1. John Wesley, *Sermons on Several Occasions*, Vol. 1 (New York: Carlton & Phillips, 1853), 177-306.

2. Günter Bornkamm, *Jesus of Nazareth*, trans. Irene and Frazer McLusky with James Robinson (New York: Harper and Row, 1960), 221.

3. Ibid., 222.

4. Rudolf Bultmann, *Theology of the New Testament*, Vol. 1, trans. K. Grobel (New York: Charles Scribner's Sons, 1951), 21.

5. Eduard Thurneysen, *The Sermon on the Mount* (Richmond: John Knox Press, 1964), 12.

6. Harvey K. McArthur, *Understanding the Sermon on the Mount* (New York: Harper & Row, 1960), 105-27.

7. W. D. Davies, *The Setting of the Sermon on the Mount* (Cambridge: Cambridge University Press, 1964). Also the abridged book by the same author, *The Sermon on the Mount* (Cambridge: Cambridge University Press, 1969).

8. David Daube, *The New Testament and Rabbinic Judaism* (London: The Athlone Press, 1956), 205-223.

Questions for Reflection

1. How do the following interpret the Sermon on the Mount?
    a. Roman Catholics
    b. Martin Luther
    c. Leo Tolstoy
    d. Albert Schweitzer
    e. Eduard Thurneysen
    f. Dispensationalists

2. In your opinion what is the meaning of the Sermon on the Mount for Christians today?

3. Point out the differences between Matthew's Sermon on the Mount and Luke' Sermon on the Plain.

4. In what way are the two sermons similar?

5. How is the Sermon on the Mount related to Mark 1:21ff.?

Chapter 1

THE BEATITUDES

Matthew 5:1-16

The Term "Beatitude"

The first eight verses of the Sermon on the Mount have through the centuries been called "beatitudes." Why are they so designated? The answer lies in the translation of certain words. In the Latin texts of the New Testament the Greek word *makarios* is commonly translated by the Latin *beatus* (singular form). Both the Greek and Latin words have the same variety of meanings such as "blessed," "fortunate," "happy," "to be congratulated," "bliss," and "hail to." At some time in the history of the Latin church the noun *beatitudo* was used to classify the eight (or nine) *beati* (plural form). Thus through a transliteration of the Latin designation *beatitudo* we call them "beatitudes."

The Septuagint, a Greek translation of the Hebrew text of the Old Testament, renders the plural construct Hebrew word *'ašrê* (pronounced "ash-reh") by the Greek word *makarios*. *'Ašrê* is used exclusively in the Psalms and Proverbs. In the Old Testament the righteous abstainers from evil, the keepers of the sabbath, and those dedicated to God were the ones saluted by "blessed," "congratulations," and other terms. While some of the Hebrews considered the congratulations as a kind of reward for obedience to God and a promise of a life of prosperity, the beatitudes did not in themselves have value, but were rather indicative of the nearness of God to those who were righteous.

Some scholars attempt to divide the Beatitudes into three groups. They contend that the first four give praise to those who are distinct from others because of a lack of something. They are the poor, mourning, meek, and hungry. Three of the four beatitudes in Luke's Gospel fall into this category. The second grouping includes the next three beatitudes that show those who are praised because they *do* specific things for humanity. They do mercy, speak truth, and make peace. The third grouping involves those who suffer persecution. This collection of types seems reasonable enough, however, the sixth beatitude, "Hail to the pure in heart" does not show activity as do the fifth and seventh. If this classification is valid then the person who submits to God's rule is characterized by what one is, what one does, and what one suffers.

The Poor in Spirit

Matthew 5:3

"Hail to the poor in spirit, because the kingdom of heaven is theirs." The parallel in Luke's Sermon on the Plain shows three distinct variations. Instead of "poor in spirit" Luke used "poor" and does not qualify it with "in spirit." In place of the third personal pronoun plural he gives the second personal pronoun plural "you." And finally, there is a change of the phrase "kingdom of heaven" in Matthew to "kingdom of God." "Poor" in Luke is a reference to economic status, while in Matthew the "poor in spirit" qualifies poverty by making it a spiritual condition. It is very definite that Luke understands the beatitudes as praise to the sure enough poor because he counters this beatitude with a woe upon the rich. But which Gospel writer followed Q? The decision is not easy to make. Many scholars believe that Luke has followed Q correctly and that Matthew made the qualification to tone down the revolutionary aspect of praise to the economically poor. Either this is the situation, or what Jesus said was based on Isaiah 61:1b where "the poor" are not clearly defined, and Matthew felt inclined to add "in spirit."

The third person used by Matthew in the beatitudes seems to be more in keeping with poetic and general diction. On the other hand the second person in Luke shows a more prosaic and direct personal concern. In Matthew Jesus progresses from an absolute proclamation (vv. 3-10) to a personal message to his disciples (vv. 11-16), and then to a statement about himself (vv. 17-19). Thus the progression is from general Old Testament witness about the character of a person God congratulates to specific utterances of Jesus.

The poor in spirit were those who recognized their own insufficiency before God and in penance regretted their way of living when they heard God's will proclaimed to them by Jesus. They were bankrupt spiritually. They were aware of a need because they were destitute. On many occasions Jesus pointed out that the religious leaders of the Jews were not aware of their destitute condition in the presence of God. Therefore he said that the harlots, sinners, and tax collectors would submit to the kingdom of God before those who were self righteous. The elder brother in the Parable of the Two Alien Sons (Luke 15:25ff.) and the Pharisee in the Parable of the Pharisee and the Tax Collector (Luke 18:10ff.) are excellent examples concerning those who believed that they had it made with God. When Jesus was denounced by the Pharisees for eating with tax collectors and sinners, the reply of Jesus was, "Those who are well have no need of a physician, but those who are sick; I came not to call the rightious, but sinners" (Mark 2:17). There seems to be a bit of irony in Jesus' reply. He saw that those who were not religiously inclined felt a need, whereas those who were extremely religious did not recognize a need.

The poor in spirit are congratulated because they have submitted to the kingdom of heaven. Matthew uses the phrase "kingdom of heaven" 33 times and the "kingdom of God" three times. In twelve instances Matthew omits God or heaven and inserts simply the word "heaven." Mark uses "kingdom of God" 14 times and in five of these cases Matthew substitutes "kingdom of heaven" for the "kingdom of God." Contrary to the claims of some who find a difference between the kingdom of God and the kingdom of heaven, the fact that Matthew substitutes "heaven" for "God" in five instances from Mark and inserts "kingdom of God" three times is an indication that he considered the phrases to be equivalent. "Heaven" is only a synonym for God. This is in keeping with Jewish aversion to overusing the name of God.

In Matthew 4:11 we observe that the author placed the beginning of Jesus' ministry in Galilee after John the Baptist was arrested. His message was a resumption of the message of John: "Repent, for the kingdom of heaven has drawn near." In verse 23 Jesus went throughout Galilee teaching in the Jewish synagogues and preaching the good news about the kingdom. Immediately thereafter he delivered the Sermon on the Mount. The close connection between the proclamation of the kingdom in Jesus' beginning ministry and the Sermon on the Mount, plus references to the kingdom in the sermon, prompts us to conclude that the whole message of the Sermon on the Mount is undergirded by the good news of the kingdom.

Varieties of opinions have been expressed concerning the nature of the kingdom of God. Social reformers, theologians, and philosophers have incorporated this phrase into their systems of thought. In the fourth century A.D. Augustine identified the kingdom of God with the church. In the last century Albrecht Ritschl defined it as a human society organized around the principle of divine love. Adolf Harnack interpreted the kingdom of God as the rule of God in the hearts of people. Johannes Weiss began, and then Albert Schweitzer continued, to stress the eschatological (last things) element in the phrase. For them the kingdom had to do with the consumation of the age in the future.

As we consider the teaching of Jesus concerning the kingdom, it is extremely difficult to shake off the influence of these views. We may say, however, that the phrase does not mean an ethical and moral attitude in the hearts of people. Jesus did not promote the idea of an earthly utopia, nor did he identify the kingdom of God with the church.

Actually, "kingdom of God" is not the most appropriate translation for the phrase Jesus used. "Reign" or "rule" of God comes closer to what Jesus meant. While some of the passages in the Gospels might appear to suggest a domain, realm, or kingdom, the vast majority of the passages indicate God's rule. In translating the phrase "rule of God," we eliminate the notion of territory to be governed. Instead we give emphasis to God's sovereignty. The dominant meaning is always that of God exercising sovereign power over humanity and the universe. God's sovereignty *is*. We do not initiate it. We do not build it up. We do not earn it. We cannot force God to give it. We do not expand or establish it. We submit to the rule of God. To be sure, we can expand the numbers of people who submit to God's sovereignty by proclamation of the good news in Jesus Christ.

Considerable debate continues among scholars as to whether the kingdom of God is present or future. We should not be too hasty and make it an "either, or" proposition. Since the kingdom of God means God's rule, quite evidently God reigns in the present and will reign in the future.

In the deeds, presence, and teachings of Jesus we understand clearly that the day of God's sovereignty has arrived. Those hopes for which the prophets had long dreamed are now present. Jesus proclaimed the good news that God's rule was present, and people must make a response to the claims of God's sovereignty. In the person of Jesus, God's rule has its greatest revelation to humanity. The acceptance or rejection of that rule is determined by the attitude of people toward Jesus. The Beatitudes clearly illustrate the characteristics of those who fully submit to the sovereignty of God.

The Mourners

Matthew 5:4

Who are these mourners? Were they lamenting their own sins or those of the Jews who were under domination of the Romans as a punishment from God for their sins? (See Isa 61:2-3). Is it the type of sorrow shown by the Jews in exile reflected in Psalm 137 and the corresponding joy of the return reflected in Psalm 126:5? The previous had to do with the national sorrow. Are they those who await the consolation of Israel as did Simeon in the temple when Mary was purified after the birth of Jesus? In Luke there is a contrast between loud weeping and merry laughter. Do they mourn because of their situation as they confront the good news proclaimed by Jesus? They throw away all of their pride and mourn because they recognize their sinful condition in the presence of God. In Judaism one did not have to shed tears in order to mourn. Mourning consisted of symbolic acts such as fasting, putting on sackcloth, sitting in ashes, screaming their sorrow, and hurting oneself. Paul mentions two kinds of sorrow. There is a grief according to God and a grief according to worldly standards. Godly sorrow produces repentance that leads to salvation, while worldly sorrow produces death (2 Cor 7:8-11).

We suppose the mourners are those who suddenly are aware of their separation from God and cry out for God to fill the vacuum in their lives. They know that they have no power to produce righteousness which will count before God, and they mourn for mercy. To those who recognize their plight congratulations are in order, because they will wipe away their tears and be comforted in the presence of God. They are not the self-satisfied, but rather recognize that they are not sufficient in themselves to merit salvation.

The Meek

Matthew 5:5

The third beatitude is a quote from Psalm 37:11. Some scholars claim that this verse should be excised from the text. It is true that some manuscripts (Bezae, 33, and Latin versions) shift its position in the order and put it between the first and second beatitudes, however, no manuscript deletes it altogether. The Hebrew words for poor (*'ānî*) and meek (*'ānāw*) are very similar. The Greek equivalent of the Hebrew word for meek is *praÿs* (pronounced "prah-ēs").

Generally we think of meekness as being that of a person similar to Caspar Milquetoast, the character made famous in a comic strip by H.T. Webster, the American cartoonist. This type of person presents an "excuse me for living" appearance. He or she is a "yes person," a wimp, shrinking, and apologetic in speech and action. In Psalm 37:11, which Jesus quotes, the meek are the gentle, the considerate, and those who are submissive to God in contrast to the wicked, the wrong doers, and those who are hostile toward God.

In Numbers 12:3 we learn that Moses was very meek. In fact he was more so than any other person. Yet on occasions he could "blow his stack" and exhibit a terrible temper. Did these violent outbursts of rage indicate that he was meek? Possibly what the author meant in describing the meekness of Moses was that he was submissive to God.

The meek in the Beatitudes are those who submit to God's sovereignty and are willing to be disciplined by God. The promise given to the meek is that "they shall inherit the earth." In Psalm 37:11 the promise of inheritance of the earth was connected with God's covenant which gave the land of Canaan to the Israelites. While the Psalmist may have had the possession of real estate uppermost in his mind, Jesus did not mean real estate. He was not embracing the idea of a new earth in a future age. He meant that those who are meek will enjoy the blessings of God's rule.

The Hungry and Thirsty

Matthew 5:6

Blessed are those who hunger and thirst after righteousness (v. 6). In contrast to Matthew, we notice that Luke simply said, "Blessed are you who hunger now, for you will be satisfied" (6:21). Luke did not add that the hunger was for righteousness. For those of us who have not faced hunger and thirst, it is hard to relate to the feelings a person might have who is starving and thirsting. In Palestine, the peasants in Jesus' day were not far from starvation. Water in certain parts of the land also was scarce. Jesus' audience had experienced both hunger and thirst and could understand what it meant to desire righteousness as one would desire food and water.

In what sense is the desire for righteousness used in verse 6? Was it a wish for God's action in the vindication of his people who had suffered from their enemies? Was it a struggle to fulfill the rigid requirements of the law and obtain an ethical righteousness? Or was it a desire to come into a right relationship with God apart from the rigid and arid legalism of Judaism? From the way Matthew used righteousness, we assume the last meaning is closer to what Jesus meant.

In the Greek language, if one says that he hungers for bread, the person normally desires a part of a loaf, not all of it. Matthew, however, used the accusative case after "hunger" and "thirst" to indicate that congratulations go to those who desire not a part of righteousness but the whole. Some people want only a partial relationship with God. They do not wish to let God's character be the pattern of their lives. Only those who hunger and thirst for total commitment will receive the praise of

God. They will be congratulated for the quest, and they will be satisfied with God's goodness.

The Merciful
Matthew 5:7

In the previous four beatitudes Jesus congratulates those who are distinct from others because of certain deficiencies. They are dispossessed of spirituality, joy, pride, and righteousness. We now move to the next three beatitudes where congratulations are in order to those who bear fruits of the life of the heart. The first of this series has to do with mercy. Jesus said, "Hail to the merciful; for they shall obtain mercy" (v.7). Does this mean that Jesus sets up a "this for that" condition? Does he say that God will show mercy to us if we show mercy to others? If so, we merit mercy because we have worked for it by being merciful. This is not the basis, however, for a sinner's hope to receive God's mercy. Mercy is a part of God's nature. His mercy is available for the merciful and the unmerciful. It is only those who exhibit mercy, however, who have fully comprehended what the mercy of God is. Unless mercy, loving kindness, and compassion flow out of a person, he or she does not really experience God's compassion, mercy, and love.

The prophet Micah centuries before had asked the question, "what does the Lord require of you?" He answered his question with, "to do justice, and to love mercy, and to walk humbly with your God" (Mic 6:8). Jesus ben Sirach, a Jewish scribe of the second century B.C., seems to be recalling the message of Micah when he says, "Does one have no mercy toward a man like himself, and yet pray for his own sins?" (Sir 28:4). Rabbi

Gamaliel, II, the Jewish Patriarch of the latter part of the first century A.D., appears to echo the same teaching when he says, "So long as you are merciful, the Merciful (i.e. God) is merciful to you" (*Tosepta Baba Qamma* 10:30).

Though Judaism of the first century A.D. accepted the teaching that a merciful God demanded that mercy be shown to others, there were Jews who refused to be merciful toward others because of a contradiction in their theology. Some believed that suffering was a direct result of sin, and they hesitated to advertise their mercy, pity, or compassion lest they obstruct the justice of God. They also were convinced that the poor were in their condition of poverty because God had not blessed them, and women who were barren no longer were approved of God. So long as they were confident that these sinners had broken God's laws, it was impossible for them to be merciful because indirectly they would be interfering with God's actions.

In like fashion the Romans clamored for justice rather than mercy. They were for justice not because a person had violated God's laws but because mercy was a sign of weakness. Stoicism, the prevailing philosophy of the day, was opposed to all emotions, but the Stoic Romans had a greater disdain for mercy.

Jesus illustrated the full meaning of mercy, forgiveness, and compassion in the Parable of the Unmerciful Servant (Matt 18:23-35). In the fifth antithetical statement in the Sermon on the Mount (5:38-42) he demands mercy rather than justice. Mercy which does not stimulate like mercy, however, must be altered into a stern demand for justice. God forgives us freely, without stint or reservation. We receive immeasurable mercy from God by God's gracious act in Jesus Christ. Having been forgiven so much, the least we can do is to forgive and be merciful to those who harm us. We should extend the same kind of patience and mercy toward them that we have received from God. A merciful attitude is essential under God's rule. To deny this attitude is to deny the nature of God.

In Shakespeare's play *The Merchant of Venice*, Portia tells Shylock that he must be merciful:

> Therefore Jew,
> Though justice be thy plea, consider this,
> That in the course of justice none of us
> Should see salvation: we do pray for mercy.
> And that same prayer doth teach us
> All to render
> The deeds of mercy.

The Pure in Heart

Matthew 5:8

The Jewish religious leaders in Jesus' day, while not ignoring inward purity, were more anxious to put the emphasis upon outward cleanliness. Before people could participate in worship they had to be ceremonially cleansed. One of the six divisions of the Mishnah, the codified oral tradition of the rabbis, is devoted to the rules of purifications. "To see God" was equivalent to the expression "appear before God." The Jewish tradition made it clear that there were certain kinds of bodily defilements which disqualified a person from worship in the temple or sharing in the observance of festivals.

Many of the Psalms considered inward purity to be essential (51:10f.; 73:1f; *et al.*). It seems, however, that the beatitude of Jesus on purity of heart is more closely related to Psalm 24.

This Psalm is a liturgy that was recited by the worshipers before entering the sanctuary of God. The question is asked, "Who shall ascend to the hill of the Lord, and who shall stand in his holy place?" (v. 3) The answer is: "He who has clean hands and a pure heart, who has not lifted up his life to what is false, and does not swear deceitfully (v. 4)." The Psalmist does not call for moral perfection or sinfulness as a prerequisite to appear before God, nor did Jesus. Should this have been the demand, no one could qualify. Jesus means that when we come before God we should be sincere, single minded, and having no mixed motives. God can trust us because we are not trying to exploit him but earnestly desire to have spiritual fellowship with him.

The teaching of this beatitude on purity of heart is further expanded in Matthew 15:1-20 (See also Mark 7:1-23). Jesus clashed with the Pharisees who citicized his disciples for not following their rules concerning ceremonial lustrations before eating. Whereupon Jesus replied, "Not what goes into the mouth defiles man, but what comes out of the mouth, this defiles a man" (v. 11). When his disciples asked for an explanation, Jesus said, "But what comes out of the mouth proceeds from the heart, and this defiles a man" (v. 18). He then enumerated the sins coming from the heart. They are evil thoughts, murder, adultery, fornication, theft, false witness, and slander.

The Peacemakers

Matthew 5:9

This beatitude comes as a comforting relief and soothing solace to all who feel that relationships in life have disintergrated and deteriorated because of wars, hostilities, antagonism, enmities, and schisms, but the saying was particularly relevant for two of Jesus' disciples. In all three Synoptic Gospels, as well as in Acts 1:13, Simon, one of the disciples, is designated to be a Zealot. We assume that Judas Iscariot, since he is usually listed with Simon the Zealot and since he betrayed the place where Jesus could be captured without a crowd present, also adhered to views of this revolutionary group. To be sure, the name Zealot was not attached to this band of cutthroats and super patriots until the time of John of Gischala in the Jewish revolt of A.D. 66-70, but these brigands who advocated revolt against the Roman domination of Palestine existed from the time of Judas the Galilean in A.D. 6. Galilee, the province in which Jesus delivered the Sermon on the Mount, was a hotbed for insurrectionists.

The Sadducees were interested in keeping the peace. Along with the high priest they were quislings of the Romans, and they were dedicated to peace in the land because if there was some outbreak of hostilities from the populace, the high priest and Sadducees were held responsible, and they faced the risk of losing their status. The Pharisees were semi-quietists who were more interested in teaching the people the Law than engaging in politics. In the rebellion of A.D. 66-70, however, they were forced against their better judgement to side with the Zealots. The famous Rabbi Hillel, who is listed in the Mishnah with 59 other teachers giving maxims in praise of the Law, said on one occasion, "Be disciples of Aaron, loving peace and pursuing peace, loving mankind and bringing them near the Law" (*Pirke Aboth* 1:12).

It is quite noticeable that this beatitude of Jesus does not congratulate those who hope for peace. Nor does Jesus commend those who are peace lovers and peace eulogizers. The congratulations go to those who *make* peace. Making peace is not passive non-resistance but action. We are to be actively engaged in reconciling people to God and reconciling people to people. God is the great Peacemaker. The Apostle Paul in Colossians 1:19-20 says, "For in him (Jesus Christ) all the fulness of God was pleased to dwell, and through him to reconcile to himself all things, whether on earth or in heaven, making peace by the blood of the cross." Again in Ephesians 2:14-15 he says of Christ, "For his is our peace, who has made us both one, and has broken down the dividing wall of hostility . . . that he might create in himself one new humanity in place of two, so making peace."

Since God is the great Peacemaker, we are called to be involved in the process of reconciliation. We are ambassadors on behalf of Christ and are ministers of reconciliation. If we are engaged in making peace, we shall be called the sons of God. If we do not, we shall be considered illegitimate for we do not portray the characteristics of a reconciling God. In the Old Testament and in Jewish tradition the title "sons of God" was a possession of Israel (Deut 14:1; Hos 1:10; Ps Sol 17:30). Those willing to be peacemakers are the genuine Israel of God.

The Persecuted

Matthew 5:10-12

The eighth of the Beatitudes in Matthew's Sermon on the Mount has to do with persecution for righteousness' sake. Jesus closed the Beatitudes with a reminder to his disciples that they could anticipate harsh treatment from others. Can we consider persecution or abuse as a blessing? But Jesus said that congratulations were in order if we suffer persecution. You will notice that not every kind of suffering merits a congratulation. It is only oppression that comes because of righteousness. Only those who experience hardship, suffering, and distress from others because they are in a right relationship with God and are submissive to his sovereignty qualify for this blessing.

Persecution invited for self-glory does not qualify for God's approval. Throughout Christian history there have been people who were killed, abused, imprisoned, maligned, and slandered, but they endured their suffering for selfish motives. They took great delight in their persecution because they wanted to appear as great heroes of the faith. Their motive was to gain a great reputation for themselves rather than glorify God. In our churches today there are people who enjoy a martyr complex. They like for people to talk about them, and they relish the feeling that comes when they are denounced. Their self-imposed persecution causes other members of the congregation to have guilt feelings and forces them to make apologies that are unjustified. As a result, those with martyr complexes can have their way from that time on because no one wants to have guilt feelings again. Martyrdom for the sake of attention does not merit a blessing.

Verse 11 is an expanded comment on persecution. In Luke 6:22 there is a list of four kinds of suffering hatred, isolation or excommunication, reproach, and slander. Matthew listed three: insult, persecution, and false accusations. Jesus did not minimize the sufferings his disciples would undergo as a result of their submission to the will of God. Suffering formed one of the themes of his earliest teachings. The danger to which his disciples would be exposed comes before us in other teachings (Matt 10:32-39; Mark 10:29-31).

In verse 10 Matthew recorded that a person had God's approval if his or her persecution was for righteousness' sake. In verse 11 he added two other conditions for congratulations. (1) The insults, oppression, and accusations heaped against an individual must be false. There is no commendation for accused persons when they are true. (2) The persecution has to be on account of Jesus. The opposition must arise from a person's Christian character and conduct.

In the midst of persecution Jesus said that we are to rejoice and be glad. Joy in suffering, however, appears to be unreasonable. One could expect bitterness, retaliation, weeping, anger, and frustration when a person is enduring insults, false accusations, isolation, and bodily harm. Certainly it is difficult to respond with joy and praise. Yet rejoicing during times of persecution was the order of the day in the early church. When the Jewish religious leaders imprisoned the apostles and later flogged them for preaching that Jesus had been raised from the dead, the apostles rejoiced because they were considered worthy to suffer dishonor in behalf of Christ (Acts 5:4). In his letter to the Philippians, Paul rejoiced in his imprisonment because it served to advance the gospel (1:12).

One of the incentives that Jesus gave for enduring persecution was a reward in heaven. The reward that Jesus meant was the full measure of God's grace. It was not public approval, a visible promotion, stars in a crown, or an appropriate return of spiritual blessing for work done. He never taught that every right deed would be matched with a corresponding reward because it was deserved. (See the Parable of the Unworthy Servant in Luke 17:7-10).

The reward of the kingdom is eternal life. Through faith in Christ we have fulfillment. The future will complete and manifest what has begun in the present. No performance on our part can give us a claim on special privileges from God. The ultimate reward is a right relationship with God by faith, not only in the present age but in the age to come. All other rewards are trivial compared to this.

A second incentive for enduring persecution is the example of the prophets. Jesus told his disciples that they were in good company if they suffered oppression for being in a right relationship with God. The prophets had undergone the same kind of rejection. Just as the prophets, with the stamp of courage on their faces, remained true to God even at the risk of their lives, so must the followers of Christ. As successors to the prophets, they must remain firm in their convictions and actions in spite of persecution.

The Salt of the Earth and the Light of the World

Matthew 5:13-16

In the last beatitude of the Sermon on the Mount (Matt 5:10-12) Jesus summoned his followers to join the prophetic company of the persecuted. Like the prophets who suffered in order to save Israel from corruption and decay, those who followed Christ were to be ready to suffer insults, abuse, and mis-reatment for telling the truth. They were to consider themselves as successors to the prophets. Jesus congratulated his disciples for remaining firm in the face of persecution. By the use of two metaphors, salt and light, he pointed out that they were destined to have a healthy and wholesome influence on humanity. As prophets of the new era, his disciples were to inspire people to higher moral living and guide them to the knowledge of God.

Verse 13 contains the first metaphor of salt. What is the nature of saltness that those of the kingdom posess? There has been much speculation among scholars concerning Jesus' meaning of salt. Some suggest that he wished to stress the preservative function of salt. Others say that he had in mind the seasoning quality of the substance. Still others believe the metaphor was a reference to the use of this element in sacrifices because of its purifying function. A few scholars, on the basis of Luke 14:35, contend that Jesus meant fertilizer and compared his disciples to salt to emphasize their life-giving quality, which people did not generally possess. All four of these functions of salt were important for the inhabitants of the first century A.D., and each function could be a suitable description of the kind of influence Jesus wanted his followers to be in the world.

But salt was normally used to preserve food. This seems to have been its most common usage. Salt as a preservative kept meat and other food products from decaying and rotting. It was a precious commodity in Jesus' day. The only way this element could preserve from corruption was to come into contact with what it was to preserve. When Jesus called his followers salt, he wanted them to understand that they were to be in the world to touch its unworthy life and redeem it. His was not a hermit-like strategy of withdrawal. His disciples were to be the element of the world that kept it wholesome and delayed God's day of judgment on a rotten society.

Righteousness is an activity of God in bringing people into a right relationship with God by the grace manifested through Jesus Christ. Because of this right relationship we follow in the character of God revealed in Jesus and possess life-preserving power for humanity. As salt of the earth we are not to escape from the world, surrender to it, compromise with it, or conform to its pattern. We are to exert our influence by coming into contact with a sinful society and be used of God to redeem it from corruption.

Concerning the follow up saying of Jesus, "If salt has lost its taste, how shall its saltiness be restored?" (v. 13b), some needlessly object that salt does not lose its nature. This is true, but under certain circumstances its salty quality can be diminished. The Jews got salt in the biblical period by evaporation in beds or pans of water along the rim of the Dead Sea or the Mediterranean. Much of the sodium chloride from the Dead Sea was mixed with other salts and was not pure.

Antiochus Epiphanes, who ruled the Seleucid Empire from 175-163 B.C., levied a tax on salt to help pay his huge war indemnities to Rome. When the Romans seized the land of Palestine in 63 B.C., the salt tax was retained. In order to make more money from their product, the salt dealers adulterated their salt; and its quality became inferior. Quite frequently salt could be soiled or mixed with dirt, and it became useless. Consequently, its usefulness as a preservative or seasoning for food was lost. Salt that has lost its salty quality is worthless.

Since salt can become useless and be discarded, Christians should beware lest they lose their essential character and become useless. If we remain aloof from the world our witness will be despised, scorned, and rejected. But if we come into contact with sinful humanity, and at the same time live a life that demonstrates obedience to God's will, we put into action an influence that is redemptive.

The second metaphor that Jesus used was light. He said, "You are the light of the world" (v. 14). This metaphor was very familiar to the Jews. The prophet Isaiah described the Servant of the Lord as a light to the nations (Isa 42:6; 49:6). In rabbinic literature the title "light of the world" was given to God, Adam, Israel, the Law, and the Temple. In his letter to the Romans the apostle Paul said that the Jews claimed they were "a light for those who are in the dark" (2:19). In John's Gospel we notice that Jesus, during the Feast of Tabernacles, proclaimed that he was "the light of the world" (8:12). In his letter to the Philippians, the apostle Paul declared that Christians are to shine as lights in the world (2:15).

When Jesus told his disciples that they were the light of the world, he laid on them a great responsibility. The recipients of God's light must become light. They were the illuminating element in the world to dispel the darkness of ignorance and sin. If their character reflected Jesus' Beatitudes, they were destined to exert a wholesome and illuminating influence on life. Jesus introduced a third metaphor to show his disciples how they must function as light. There are two ways to obtain safety. A person can take up a commanding position or go into hiding. Jesus prefered the former because he wanted his disciples to be visible, like a city on a hill.

The Essenes in the community of Qumran called themselves the "sons of light," but they isolated themselves from society. Jesus, to the contrary, warned his followers that while their relation to the outside world might be full of suffering, they should remain in the world.

In verse 15, Jesus, in a whimsical manner, says that people just do not put a lamp under a bowl. Light is useful only as it is seen. How ridiculous it is for someone to hide a lamp under some sort of covering! The purpose of a lamp is to give light, and if it is not used in this way, why have a lamp? As light we are to shine before people. Christian character is not individual and selfish but social and beneficial to others. As light we enlighten those who live in darkness to the way of truth and to the source of life. We dispel darkness of evil and bring order into the world. By our own lives we can show what true life is.

Jesus did not command us to be salt or light. He assumed that we were salt *and* light. We cannot be his followers and be deficient in these qualities. As salt, however, it is imperative that we *preserve*, and as light, it is demanded of us to *shine*. Later in the Sermon on the Mount Jesus warned his disciples about self-seeking in almsgiving, prayer, and fasting. Here he urged his followers to shine as lights before others so that others could see their good works. Did Jesus contradict himself? Not at all. In almsgiving, prayer, and fasting he condemned the hypocrites who did these acts of piety for self-glory. In verse 16 he exhorted the disciples to show genuineness in character so that our works will give God glory. The difference is between self-glory and glory to God.

Questions for Reflection

1. Why do we call the sayings of Jesus in Matthew 5:3-12 by the title Beatitudes?

2. Who are the poor in spirit?

3. What did Jesus mean by the phrase “the kingdom of God”? What are some mistaken notions as to the meaning of the phrase?

4. Is there any difference between the kingdom of God and the kingdom of heaven?

5. Who are the meek?

6. Do we receive mercy from God strictly on the basis of our being merciful to others?

7. What does it mean to be pure in heart?

8. Is passive resistance to be equated with being a peacemaker?

9. Under what conditions do we receive God’s commendation when we are persecuted?

10. Explain the metaphors “salt of the earth” and the “light of the world” as they apply to Christians?

Chapter 2

THE SIX CONTRASTS

Matthew 5:17-48

Part One: Jesus' Attitude toward the Law

After giving the Beatitudes to illustrate the characteristics of those who submit to the rule of God, and after calling on his disciples to be a preservative element in society, as well as a shining light in their righteousness, Jesus clarified his opinion of the Mosaic law. Presumably this was done in order to clear up any misunderstanding about the six anti-antithetical sayings that were to follow.

The Preamble to the Contrasts

Through the years the preamble to the six contrasts has caused many New Testament scholars to raise a number of questions.

(1) Did Jesus utter these words, or did Matthew insert them because he was writing to a Jewish Christian community that still upheld the law?

(2) If verse 17 is from the lips of Jesus, what did he mean by "fulfill" the law?

(3) Is not verse 18 a more stringent view of the Scriptures than that of the Pharisees?

(4) Does verse 19 look back to verses 17-18 or forward to the antithetical sayings?

Those who raise the first question maintain that these verses should be excluded from the Sermon on the Mount because they appear to be an invention of Matthew. The material does not occur in Mark, and only verse 18 is found in Luke. On the surface it might seem that Matthew has taken these verses from Q, a source used by both Matthew and Luke, but Luke chose to record only one of the verses in 16:17. A close scrutiny, however, shows that verse 18 is not the equivalent of Luke 16:17. Therefore Matthew is alone in the recording of the preamble to the six contrasts.

The second question pertains to the meaning of verse 17. If Jesus did not abrogate the law and the prophets, what did he mean by fulfilling them? The Greek word for fulfill (*plēroō*) has a variety of meanings. It means: (1) to complete in detail; (2) to cause to stand and confirm the true meaning; (3) to make true what has been said or promised; (4) to establish; and (5) to fill up in measure. There would be no difficulty in understanding what Jesus said concerning fulfilling the law and prophets if verses 18-19 had not been inserted. These verses make Jesus take a more literalistic stand on the law than the Pharisees. To be sure Jesus upheld certain portions of the law, but it is very clear from the illustrations which follow in the contrasts that he did not support or endorse the literalistic interpretations of the law espoused by the Pharisees.

Of the meanings given to *plēroō* it seems that "establish" is most accurate in this context. Some scholars believe that the Aramaic word *kayyêm* is the reason for the use of this Greek word. *Kayyêm* means "to establish or to uphold." In a second century A.D. Midrash (commentary) on Exodus Rabbi Pappias said, "Man has become as one of us" (Gen 3:22).[1] He interpreted this to signify that God likens man to angels. His contemporary Rabbi Akiba rejected the opinion of Pappias. As a consequence Pappias replied, "How then do you uphold (*kayyêm*) this verse?" Akiba abruptly responded, "Man has become one of two ways, the evil one of his choice." The Hebrew text of Genesis 3:22 has *mimmennû* (of us) though it could also be *mimmennô* (of himself). Akiba used *mimmennô* and consequently upheld his doctrine of the evil and good impulses by exchanging the place of a dot on the Hebrew *waw*. How did Jesus uphold the law and the prophets, if in three of the antithetical sayings he did, in fact, invalidate the law? Jesus began where the law stood, but he brought out the spirit of the law by stressing the intention of God behind the letter. He chose to go beyond the scribal minutiae and affirm the genuine will of God by expressing his own insights. Jesus dared to make a distinction between the will of God and the expression of that will in the law. Paul in Romans 3:31 contended before his imaginary objectors that he upheld the law. Admittedly another Greek word is used, but it is equivalent to the rabbinic *kayyêm*. How does he establish the law? He accomplished this by using one of Hillel's principles of interpretation known as the *Gezerah Shawah* and in turn reversing the *Gezerah Shawah*. This principle involved drawing analogies from passages on the basis of link words. By this method Paul proved that a right relationship with God had always been on the basis of faith.

Is verse 18 more stringent than the opinion of the Pharisees toward Scripture? It certainly appears to be. The saying preserves the permanent validity of the law to the very letter. Shall we accuse Jesus of being a literalist? Yet on the other hand he taught contrary to certain portions of the law. Could this be another hyperbole of Jesus, like "a camel going through the eye of a needle," or "straining out the gnat and swallowing a camel?" It is possible that he had reference to the Torah (law) as divine instruction rather than the multitude of community rules or rituals of the Pentateuch and rabbinic oral tradition. If so, Jesus was concerned less for each little precept and more interested in the essential core which did have permanent validity.

The Context of the Contrasts

It would be to our advantage to know the context in which verse 18 was originally delivered, rather than depend upon Matthew's arbitrary collection of materials that make up the Sermon on the Mount. We have already noted that Luke contains a similar saying, but there are some differences as well (16:17). If we could say that there was some sort of continuity in Luke 16, though this is very difficult to affirm, the immediate context of Luke 16:17 is a denunciation of the Pharisees by Jesus. Therefore, Jesus was condemning the stringency of the scribes with respect to Scripture and was not supporting the permanency of the law when he said, "But it is easier for heaven and earth to pass away, than for one dot of the law to fall" (v. 17).

Does verse 19 look back to verses 17-18 or forward to the antithetical sayings? Are the commandments in verse 19 equivalent to law in the previous verses? The grammatical structure favors the commands which follow rather than the commandments in verses 17 and 18. The writer should have used "those" instead of "these" if his reference was to the previous verses. Over sixty years ago Montefiore, a famous Jewish scholar, made a very helpful suggestion.[2] He proposed the possibility of verses 19 and 20 being originally another contrast. The antithesis would run like this,

> Whoever abrogates one of the smallest commands in the law shall be called least in the kingdom of heaven, and whoever does and teaches them shall be called greatest in the kingdom of heaven, but I say to you that unless your righteousness excels that of the scribes and Pharisees . . .

Montefiore's observation is indeed very fascinating, but we have no manuscript evidence to support the conclusion. It seems to me that if there was an antithesis here, it would include verses 18-20.

In the conclusion to the preamble to the six contrasts Jesus reads, "For I tell you, unless your righteousness exceeds that of the scribes and Pharisees, you will never enter the kingdom of heaven" (v. 20). Probably the most religious men who ever lived were the Pharisees. They were very conscientious in trying to follow the commands of God. They were strict observers of the most minute details of the law. They supposed that this punctiliousness in adhering to God's demands was righteousness. They studied the law so that they would be in close contact with the intention of God, but, sad to say, they never discovered it. Their obedience to God was measurable by deeds which in turn accrued into capital gains. The law became a roof to shelter them from the penetrating light of God's will. God was hidden behind the law, and they concealed themselves from God behind a wall of works and achievements.

Jesus told his disciples that their righteousness must surpass the kind shown by the Pharisees if they wished to be submissive to God's will. What kind of righteousness excels that of the religious leaders of Jesus' day? It is quite clear from the beatitudes and what follows in the Sermon on the Mount what kind of righteousness Jesus had in mind. Genuine righteousness comes from within the individual. It stems from the inner life which has been transformed by the power of God. It is an inner purity of character, and an outward display of that inner purity. The outward manifestation is consistent with the inner character of the person. By submitting to God's sovereignty we display mercy, love, peace, honesty, sincerity, purity, and humility. When we come into contact with society, we are to be what we are in the presence of God.

Verse 20 seems to introduce us to the antithetical sayings in chapter five and continues with its emphasis through verse 18 of the sixth chapter. The kind of righteousness that exceeds the righteousness of the Pharisees is seen on the horizontal level of person relationships in the contrasts that are made. On the vertical level of our relationship with God, we are to excel the Pharisees religious acts of piety (6:1-18).

The Pattern of the Six Contrasts

All of the antithetical sayings follow more or less this particular pattern, "You have heard it was said by them of old, but I say to you." The first clause gives a scriptural rule narrowly interpreted, and the second clause proposes a wider demand by Jesus. Jesus went back to the spirit and heart of the commandments for his interpretation.

The rabbis had a formula similar to the one used by Jesus, but it was stated in reverse order. They said, "I might hear or understand the literal meaning in Scripture to be such and such, but you must say." A good example of this form is found in a commentary on Exodus which represents the interpretation of the school of Ishmael in the second century A.D. In an exposition of the fifth commandment in Exodus 20:12 the rabbis remarked: "I might understand the command to mean honor with words only." They went on to say that Proverbs 3:9 used the same Hebrew word for honor, and in that context the word meant to honor with substance. Thus the rabbis concluded that honor in the fifth commandment also pertained to food, drink, and clothing.

The Pharisees believed that if they kept the text of the law, as interpreted by itself or tradition, they were accepted by God. This was a limited concept of obedience. When a person obeyed a literal command, he or she could feel secure and pretend to keep the evil desire isolated from himself or herself. In the event that a Jew went beyond what the law proposed, this act of itself earned favor and merit with God.

Jesus refused to accept this scheme of things. He could not tolerate the use of the law as a screen to ward off the fullness of God's revelation. He forced the Jewish leaders to examine their inner life of thoughts, desires, and motives. He taught that God searches us and reveals our wickedness. He destroys our contentment with self and makes us depend completely on the grace and mercy of God.

The rabbis taught that God's judgment depended on what a person did or did not do. Jesus insisted that the ultimate test is the character of the person. While it is true that actions reveal character, as Jesus indicated in Matthew 7:16, actions do not reveal all about human nature and disposition. God alone knows this. In each of the antithetical sayings before us, Jesus demanded a radical transformation of character, attitude, and disposition.

Part Two: The First Three Contrasts

The Sanctity of Life *Matthew 5:21-26*

Jesus spoke to the common people who were generally illiterate. The Scriptures were in Hebrew, the language of the scholars. The rabbis read from the Old Testament in Hebrew before the congregation in the synagogue, but they depended on a translator to present the Aramaic paraphrase so the people could understand what was written. Thus it was appropriate for Jesus to say, "You have heard," rather than, "You have read."

The first contrast upholds the sanctity of life. Jesus referred to the sixth commandment of the Decalogue which stressed the sacredness of human life by prohibiting murder (Exod 20:13; Deut 5:17). The latter part of the clause "anyone who murders will be subject to judgment" (v. 21) is based on the written law (Lev 24:17; Deut 17:8-13). "Subject to Judgement" signifies that a person was liable to trial and punishment prescribed by the law. The person charged with murder was brought before the Sanhedrin, the ecclesiastical and civil court of the Jews. If convicted, the accused was put to death.

The Old Testament prophets pronounced their oracles with "thus says the Lord." The Pharisees claimed that they were the successors to the prophets, but they were not so bold to say that they received their authority directly from God. They appealed to the sages, the majority opinion of the rabbis, or their own ordination as a sufficient source of power to make declarations. Theirs was a derived authority. In contrast to the Pharisees Jesus made and declared his decisions on his own authority. Thus he was able to say, "But I tell you."

Jesus went beyond the simple statement of the law's demand to declare the intention of God who gave the commandment. He condemned not only the overt act of murder, but also the inner attitude from which the act originated. He was as much concerned for the causes as he was for the consequences of sinful acts. The courts addressed themselves to the prohibited act, which was the end of the process. But Jesus went back to the motivation and thoughts that produced the deed. He considered coddled anger as incipient murder. He said, "Anyone who is angry with his brother will be subject to judgment." The King James Version says, "Whoever is angry with his brother without cause." "Without cause" appears in a few reliable manuscripts as well as in quotations from the Fathers. The earliest manuscripts, however, do not have this reading. The insertion suggests that a later scribe found the teachings of Jesus too strong for him.

In 1 John 3:15 the author of the epistle undoubtedly was aware of the teaching of Jesus on anger in the Sermon on the Mount when he said, "Anyone who hates his brother is a murderer." Rabbi Eliezer, a teacher of the first century A.D. was in agreement with Jesus when he said, "He who hates his neighbor, behold, he belongs to the shedders of blood." The kind of anger Jesus was talking about was not a sudden burst of rage that soon exhausted itself. The word used by Matthew is *orgizomenos* which means a seething type of anger. It is a wrath which is nursed to keep it warm. It is an anger over which a person broods and will not allow to go away.

The consequence of anger is judgment. What kind of judgment did Jesus have in mind? Some scholars believe that he referred to judgment in the local courts. But the Jewish tribunals, just like the courts today, had no jurisdiction over a person who was angry. They could address themselves only to the overt act produced by anger. The judiciary had no sure way of knowing the inner feelings, thoughts, and motives of a person. There seems to be no doubt that Jesus indicated divine judgment. Only God can properly judge a person's disposition. He alone would have the knowledge needed.

Verses 22b-26 are an expansion of the antithetical statement on murder. The content is closely related to verses 21-22a. Thus the antithesis lies in the contrast between the external act of murder, which was under the jurisdiction of the courts, and the inward disposition which is under the jurisdiction of God. By rabbinic and worldly standards a good person is one who does not commit an overt act to disobey the law. By Jesus' standard no individual is good until the disposition to do what is forbidden is changed. Jesus extended the scope of the law against murder and included within the sweep of its prohibition not only the overt act but the attitude. Murder is not just stabbing, shooting, or poisoning a person. Hatred is a type of murder. The actual deed stems from harboring a bitter resentment, keeping the fires of wrath burning, bearing grudges, and seeking revenge.

In addition to anger Jesus included contempt and abuse. To call a brother a *raka* was a cause for litigation. The person who used this word against someone else was liable to the Sanhedrin, the Jewish court. It is not certain what this Aramaic word signified. Some suppose that it is to be identified with the rabbinic word *rêqâ*–meaning "good for nothing." At any rate it was an insulting word. Insults under Jewish law were looked upon as downgrading one's humanity. The Sanhedrin declared it mandatory that reparations in money be made to the injured party. Apparently calling a brother a fool was not a basis for litigation in the courts. The word used here is *mōre*. In rabbinic literature the Greek word is transliterated as *moreh*, and for the sages it meant stubborn. Nevertheless, it was some sort of abusive word, and whoever used it against a brother was liable to God's judgment.

It is doubtful that verses 23-26 are a part of the first antithetical saying. The last two verses have a parallel in Luke 12:57-59, but verses 23-24 do not appear in Mark or Luke. Matthew must have decided that these sayings were relevant to the subject at hand. The subject is reconciliation. Jesus declared that reconciliation takes precedence over worship in the Temple. Peaceful relations must be maintained at all costs. If an individual should go to the Temple to present his offering, and there remembers that his brother has feelings against him he is to take the initiative in making peace with his brother before making his offering. In Judaism if a person wronged his neighbor, he must ask forgiveness of the one wronged before God would forgive him. In Jesus' teaching it is the person who is wronged that seeks reconciliation. Rabbi Eleazar ben Azariah, a sage of the second century A.D. said: "For transgressions that are between man and God the Day of Atonement effects atonement; but for transgressions that are between man and his fellow the Day of Atonement effects atonement only if he has appeased his fellow."[3]

The Sanctity of Marriage *Matthew 5:27-30*

The second contrast is introduced by reciting the seventh commandment of the Decalogue which was a prohibition of adultery (Exod 20:14; Deut 5:18). In Jewish law adultery was sexual intercourse between a married woman and a man other than her husband. The Jews also taught that if a woman was betrothed to a man and had sexual intercourse with a man other than her betrothed, she was guilty of adultery. The rule that applied to the wife did not apply to the husband. In Judaism the husband did not commit adultery against his wife or against a woman to whom he was engaged. The unfaithful husband only committed adultery against his lover's husband.

In verse 28 Jesus supplemented the seventh commandment with the tenth commandment which was against coveting. As in the case of murder, he made a distinction between the overt act of adultery and the inward attitude that produced the act. The law of adultery was given to protect the sanctity of marriage. Jesus expanded the seventh commandment to include lust and, by this addition, enhanced the purity of the man-woman relationship. The burning desire of a man to have sexual intercourse with a woman other than his wife shows what kind of person is within. In the eyes of God such a person is an adulterer. The rabbis also declared that lust was a breach of the seventh commandment. They said that if anyone looked at a woman to desire her, he committed unlawful intercourse with her.

While the sin of adultery was specifically limited to those who were married, Jesus seems to include fornication in verse 28 by warning his disciples about the lustful look at any woman. Both adultery and fornication are extreme forms of a desire to violate the personality of another. In love there is recognition of responsibility to correspond to the privilege of sex. In lust there is the desire to use a person selfishly and irresponsibly. Today we speak of viewing someone as a sex object rather than a person in God's image. Love for a person excludes using him or her to pander to one's lust.

Verses 29-30 are similar to Mark 9:43-48 and Matthew 18:8-9. It is quite possible that Matthew decided to incorporate these verses from his dependence on Marcan material and place them after verse 28 because he thought the teaching was relevant to lust. The order in Mark is hand, foot, and eye. Matthew mentions only the eye and the hand, omitting the foot. Matthew seems to connect the eye with the lustful look.

In Judaism the right hand was of greater value than the left hand. By assimilation Matthew gave the same value to the right eye. Sight and touch with the hand stimulate passions. With this rhetorical exaggeration Jesus was telling his disciples that a blemish in any part of the body might contaminate the whole. Sin in any part of the person needs to be conquered before it spreads throughout one's life.

We are not to suppose that the words of Jesus should be taken literally. Very few Christians have done so in the history of the Church. If a person should go so far as to pluck out the right eye, the left eye remains for lustful looking. The person who cuts off his right hand still possesses feeling in the left hand. Even if one is blind, passion has not been removed. Jesus sought purity in heart, and he taught that no sacrifice was too great or painful to achieve this goal.

Divorce *Matthew 5:31-32*

In the third antithetical saying of Jesus the introductory formula, "You have heard that it was said" is noticeably abbreviated to simply, "It was said" (v.31). This contrast has to do with divorce. The "it was said" is a reference to Deuteronomy 24:1 which says,

> When a man takes a wife and marries her, if then, she finds no favor in his eyes because he has found some indecency in her, and he writes her a bill of divorce and puts it in her hands and sends her out of the house . . .

Thus the Deuteronomic code allows divorce on the basis of some inadequacy or an unseemly practice.

In the first century A.D. both groups of Pharisees, the school of Shammai and the school of Hillel, allowed divorce on the basis of the teaching of Deuteronomy 24:1. Those who embraced the view of Shammai were more stringent in their ruling. For them the grounds for divorce were only in the case of adultery which they interpreted as an unseemly practice. Those who followed Hillel were more liberal. Hillel himself said that a man may divorce his wife "even if she spoiled a dish for him" (*Mishnah Gittin* 9:10). In the same reference in the Mishnah we note that Akiba, a rabbi of the second century A.D., said that if a man found a woman more beautiful than his wife, he had grounds for divorce. As evidence he quoted that part of Deuteronomy 24:1 that says, "And it shall be if she finds favor in his eyes."

This saying on divorce attributed to Jesus in the Sermon on the Mount has parallels in Mark 10:11-12 and Luke 16:18. The saying of Jesus occurs again in Matthew 19:9f. In both of the references in Matthew an exception clause has been inserted. For many years this exception clause has been viewed by scholars with great suspicion. It is considered spurious for many reasons. (1) Since Jesus did not give exceptions in other matters but set forth absolutes, it is very doubtful that he did in this instance. (2) Mark and Luke seem to know nothing of divorce allowable for unchastity. (3) Paul in 1 Corinthians 7:10-16 is not aware of the exception clause. (4) In the light of Jesus' total teachings, it does not appear that he would condone divorce on the basis of unlawful sexual intercourse as long as the guilty person asked for forgiveness. (5) In Matthew 19:10 the reply of Jesus' disciples to his teaching on divorce was, "If such is the case of a man with his wife, it is not expedient to marry." This of itself indicates that Jesus set forth the absolute, which was no divorce. Otherwise, the disciples would not have been so shocked. (6) Finally, there would be no reason for Jesus to say that Deuteronomy 24:1 was not the intention of God but came in as a concession to the people because previous to the command a wife could be dismissed without a reason and thus violate her rights.

At any rate when the Pharisees in Matthew 19:3 asked Jesus, "Is it lawful to divorce one's wife for any reason?" it is clear that they were trying to put him on the spot to force an agreement with Hillel or Shammai. By inserting the exception clause, the author has put Jesus on the side of Shammai. The rest of what Jesus said, however, does not coincide with this opinion. In the remainder of the conversation Matthew follows Mark. The Pharisees wanted to know why Moses permitted divorce. The response of Jesus was that Deuteronomy 24:1 was not the intention of God but a concession on the part of Moses due to the hardness of heart among the Israelites. Up until the time of the Deuteronomic code, a man could tell his wife to hit the road for no reason at all. The implication is that Deuteronomy 24:1 was a protection of the rights of women against capricious men.

Jesus then appealed to Genesis 1:27 and 2:24 to show that it was the intention of God from the very beginning that there should be unity in marriage. To the purpose of God for marriage in the creation accounts, Jesus added, "What therefore God has joined together, man is not to sever" (v.6). On the basis of what Jesus said here, the exception clause in 19:9 does not coincide at all with the divine intention. This clause reduces the absolute to a relative.

As to the consequences relative to divorce, there are some differences between Matthew and Mark. Mark 10:11 has, "Whoever divorces his wife and marries another commits adultery against her." This was not in accord with Jewish law for if a man divorced his wife and married another, he committed adultery against the man who was previously married to her. Never did the Jews consider that a man committed adultery against his wife. In Matthew 5:32 if a man married a divorced woman, he committed adultery. Is it against his divorced wife or against the man who divorced his wife? The text is not clear on this point. Matthew 19:9 does not include marrying a divorced woman, but simply says that if a man "marries another, he commits adultery." The inference is that the man married a woman who was single. In this case there would be agreement with Mark that the man committed adultery against his divorced wife. Luke is also in agreement with Matthew 19:9 and 5:32b (Luke 16:18).

Matthew 5:32b contains something not in Mark. If a man divorced his wife, he made the wife an adulteress. The author of Matthew's Gospel, however, added the exception to the rule. If a man's wife was guilty of illicit sexual intercourse, he did not make his wife an adulteress because she was already in that condition. Yet if she was not guilty, the husband through divorce made the woman an adulteress in the eyes of the public. Thus the husband bore the full moral responsibility for the state of affairs of the wife.

In Jewish law the wife was not allowed to divorce her husband, yet Mark has Jesus saying, "If she divorces her husband and marries another, she commits adultery" (10:12). It is true that in certain cases a wife could force her husband to divorce her, but it was never proper in Judaism to say that a woman could divorce her husband. Admittedly, there were a few exceptions. We know from the Elephantine papyri that a Jewish colony in Egypt permitted a wife to divorce her husband, but this cannot be cited as an orthodox practice in Judaism because this colony of Jews was unorthodox in the way that they practiced their religion.

Though there are some discrepancies in the Synoptic Gospels concerning Jesus' teaching about divorce, the main issue has to do with the rights of women. In Judaism the wife was viewed as nothing more than property, and the husband was in full control. The wife was subjected to the personal whims, caprices, and vagaries of a kink-in-the-brain husband. In his teaching on divorce, Jesus emerges as a champion for the cause of women.

Part Three: The Other Contrasts

Oaths *Matthew 5:33-37*

The fourth contrast of Jesus is about oaths. The "you have heard" is not an exact citation of the Old Testament. It is a conflation or a summary of Leviticus 19:12, Exodus 20:7, Numbers 30:2f, and Deuteronomy 5:11 and 23:22. All of these verses are directly or indirectly connected with the third commandment. The Hebrews were allowed to call upon God as a witness to assure others that they would complete their vows and also be truthful in any testimony they gave. They were cautioned, however, to be certain that they fulfilled their oaths and told the truth; otherwise, their vows meant nothing and their credibility was questioned. In addition, and this was more sinful, they held little regard for God by whom they swore. Consequently, the character of God was dishonored by them.

The rabbis tried to dissuade the Jews from taking an oath which they could not keep. They also taught that only an oath was binding when the person swore in the name of God. This gave rise to the Jews taking an oath and circumventing the name of God. They could swear by objects relating to worship such as the Temple, the gold of the Temple, the altar, or heaven. It was a principle of casuistry. But this misled the people into believing that some oaths were not binding. At the same time the evasion gave the vows a sort of religious coloration as though they were binding. By allowing the people to circumvent the command on oaths, the rabbis set up a double standard of credibility. Since they required a person to tell the truth when an oath was taken, then that person was free to tell a lie if not under oath.

Contrary to what the law and the teachings of the rabbis permitted, Jesus banned all oaths. By doing this he abrogated the law concerning oaths. Instead of vows Jesus set forth the principle of absolute truthfulness. He denounced the evasions of the law on swearing which used heaven, earth, Jerusalem, or one's head as a substitute for God's name and indicated that all of these imply a reference to God. When a person says, "I swear," it is implied that God has been called down as a witness to his or her credibility. When a person is honest, all oaths are superfluous. The word of a truthful individual is more trustworthy than the word of a liar even though the liar should embellish it with the most solemn oath. Anyone who has a reputation for honesty does not need an oath to decorate his or her veracity.

Josephus, the Jewish historian of the first century A.D., tells us that the Jewish sect of Essenes was noted for fidelity, and what they said was firmer than an oath.[4] He went on to say that they shunned oaths, which they considered to be worse than perjury, and contended that if one could not be trusted to tell the truth without an oath that person was already condemned. The Essenes did permit an exception to their rule. When a candidate was admitted to the formal organization of the community, he had to commit himself to a binding oath.[5]

Today we might not find in Christian circles those who would swear by God to keep a vow or to tell the truth, but there are circumventions which are just as ridiculous. There are those who hoodwink the community into believing that they are telling the truth. They use such expressions as "God revealed to me to do this or that," "It is God's will that we embark on this venture," or "If I don't raise a certain amount of money, God is going to kill me." Some religious leaders think that they have received an authority from God through ordination and that this of itself is a validation of their integrity. God's name is degraded by these claims because the character of God becomes a mockery among believers.

Retaliation *Matthew 5:38-42*

The fifth antithetical saying of Jesus begins at verse 38. It is noticeable that a reference is not made to a commandment from the Decalogue. Rather Jesus goes back to the law of retaliation found in Exodus 21:22-25, Leviticus 24:19-21, and Deuteronomy 19:21. In all three of these passages the law of retaliation begins with "life for a life." Interestingly enough Jesus omits the "life for a life" phrase while including "eye for an eye" and "a tooth for a tooth." It is understandable that the phrase was omitted by Jesus because capital punishment was a matter for the courts to adjudicate. He was only interested in injuries which could be settled among individuals in their personal relationships.

Limited retaliation was a tremendous improvement over bedouin blood revenge in primitive society. Under retaliation the injured person was restricted in the amount of punishment that could be inflicted. The punishment could not exceed the amount received. In Jesus' day the Pharisees had already rejected the law of retaliation. The measure for measure rule did not apply. If personal injuries were committed, the injured party claimed reparations instead of injury in kind to the offender. The compensation included damages for pain, medical treatment, and loss of time from work. The Sadducees retained the law of retaliation.

Like the Pharisees, Jesus abrogated the tit for tat rule, but he went beyond the teachings of the Pharisees by ruling out reparations for injuries received. He set forth an attitude which was more in keeping with proper relations to others. He presented five examples to show the disciples how they were to respond when wronged. All of the actions proposed by Jesus were positive in nature and not negative.

(1) If someone strikes you on the right cheek, turn to him the other also. To hit a person on the right cheek was not a harmful blow physically. How can a man punch another on the right cheek unless he is left-handed? The backhanded slap on the right cheek was a form of insult. In rabbinic writings we

learn that an insulting slap on the face deserved more compensation than a slap with intent to do physical harm. For physical injury an aggressor had to pay 200 *zuz* , yet for a backhanded slap and other forms of insult a man was required to pay 400 *zuz*, (a rabbinic term, equal to one half of a shekel; also called a *denar*).

Turning the other cheek is not passive resistance but aggressive love. Jesus insisted that we should not stand on our rights and claim reparations for wrongs committed against us. When we are insulted we are to show mercy rather than resort to litigation. Jesus called for mercy not justice. The law of equity cannot reconcile damaged relationships among people. It only enhances the estrangement between persons. We have to concern ourselves with the attitudes and dispositions of those who insult us. This requires more than measure for measure or saving face. This is a way of life which calls for Christian love, mercy, and compassion.

(2) What if someone wants to sue you? The second illustration is a case before civil court. Someone enters a suit against a person and gets a tunic in settlement. Jesus said that under these conditions the person sued should give his cloak as well. Under Jewish law the cloak of an individual was exempt from litigation because it served as a covering and provided protection from cold weather. Jesus was saying that we should not stand on our legal rights but go beyond what the law requires.

(3) What if you were pressed into service? The third example is a reference to the Roman practice of impressing civilians into service for the government. The Persians instituted the system, and it was copied by the Romans. The situation assumed by Jesus is that of a Jew impressed into service as a baggage carrier for a Roman soldier of the army of occupation.

If one of his disciples should be forced into service, Jesus said that he should double what was demanded. Instead of carrying the baggage one mile, one should take it two miles. In this way he asserted his freedom by going above and beyond what the law demanded.

(4) What if someone begs you for something? This example, as well as the fifth, is the most difficult to understand. What traveler in the Middle East has not heard the cry of "*Bakhsheesh*"? In that area of the world, begging is a way of life for many people. The same situation existed in Jesus' day. Some people made a profession of begging. To give to them encouraged deceit and idleness. To be sure, some were in desperate need of food and clothing. Begging, however, is an institution that downgrades a person. Possibly what Jesus meant was that a person was not forced by law to give to a beggar, but the gift was an act of mercy and love. We show our freedom by giving out of compassion rather then by compulsion.

(5) What if someone wants a loan? The last illustration is about a person who asks for a loan. The law could not force a person to grant a loan to a neighbor. Again Jesus was saying that we must exercise our freedom and give a loan out of compassion. We may not encounter situations today that correspond in detail to the illustrations given by Jesus. What we do see in the examples is the kind of attitude we should have in relating to others. We are not to stand on our rights and fight for strict justice, but we are to be merciful and overcome evil with good.

Love of Enemies *Matthew 5:43-48*

The last antithetical saying of Jesus in the Sermon on the Mount is, "You have heard that it was said, 'Love your neighbor and hate your enemy'; but I tell you, Love your enemies and pray in behalf of those who persecute you." The command to love one's neighbor was well-known in Judaism, but "hate your enemy" did not occur anywhere in the Old Testament as a command. Some scholars suggest that the two clauses were joined together as a popular maxim in Judaism. Others believe that "hate your enemy" was inferred from the experiences of oppression by the Jews at the hands of their conquerors who hated God. Therefore, the Jews reasoned that those who hated God must be hated by God. If God hated his enemies, they were required to do the same.

The Jews stretched the command to love one's neighbor so that it could include the proselyte and resident alien in Palestine. But Jesus widened the circle of love to include enemies as well. He swept away all quibbling over distinctions between neighbors and enemies and commanded us to love all people. Love is not only a commitment of one's whole personality (thought, feeling, and will) to the best interests of another in spite of a hostile attitude toward us, but it also prompts us to pray in behalf of those who oppress us. We are to use our highest means of communication with God for the benefit of those who would do us harm.

Jesus gave three reasons why we should love our enemies and pray for those who persecute us. The first is that God's love is universal. He loves all people without any distinction (v. 45). Secondly, Jesus' disciples were to demonstrate a righteousness higher than that of the tax collectors and Gentiles, to say nothing of the Pharisees (v. 46-47). The third reason, but by no means the least, was that the disciples were to be like God in their love. They were summoned to reflect the character of God by refusing to be discriminatory in their love. As disciples of one who embodied the love of God, they were to be mature in their expression of love, which means to love as God loves.

The normal requirement for decent living is to love those who love us, but Jesus demanded that we love those who hate us. We are to be complete in our love as God is complete. Such a kind of love shows that we are, indeed, the children of God.

The Greeks had four words that meant love. Unfortunately in the English language we have only one word for love. We can love hot dogs, Chevrolets, apple pie, as well as people. We know that the word "like" should be used in place of love, but we take the popular expression whether it is right or not. The four Greek words for love were *eros*, *philia*, *storgē*, and *agapē*. *Eros* was generally used to describe sexual love or love for a adorable object, but sometimes it was employed to express friendship love. *Philia* was restricted to love for a friend. *Storgē* usually meant love of parents for their children, but frequently conveyed the meaning of patriotic love—the love for one's fatherland. *Agapē* was a colorless word that was seldom used, however, it was this word for love that the early Christians accepted to express God's relationship to us, our relationship to God, and our relationship to others. *Agapē* is the word selected in verses 43–46 as well as other sections of the New Testament to summon us to seek the best interests of others. The apostle Paul vividly expresses the characteristics of *agapē* in I Corinthians 13.

Endnotes

1. *Mekhilta* on Exodus 14;2.

2. C.G. Montefiore, *Rabbinic Literature and Gospel Teachings* (London: Macmillan & Co., 1930), 38.

3. *Mishnah Yoma* 8.9.

4. Flavius Josephus, *Wars of the Jews*, 2.8.6.

5. Dead Sea Scrolls, *Manual of Discipline*, 5:8.

Questions for Reflection

1. What was probably the original context for the Preamble to the Antitheses?

2. What did Jesus mean when he told his disciples that their righteousness must exceed that of the scribes and Pharisees?

3. Upon what authority did Jesus base his right to make assertions that went beyond the wording of the law of Moses?

4. Why did Jesus point to anger as an offense equal in seriousness to murder?

5. How was adultery defined in Jesus' day?

6. Which Jewish interpretation of the law's provision for divorce did Jesus' view resemble the most? How did his view differ from this position?

7. How were oaths used by Jews in Jesus' day?

8. What was the original intention of the "eye for an eye" principle?

9. What limitations may be placed on Jesus' command to love the enemy?

Chapter 3

WORSHIP: A MORE EXCELLENT WAY

Matthew 6:1–18

Recognizing the Perils of Piety

In Matthew 5:20 Jesus said, "Unless your righteousness surpasses that of the Pharisees and the teachers of the law, you will certainly not enter the kingdom of heaven." In the verses that follow this saying (2–48) Jesus explained how this righteousness was to excel the righteousness of the Pharisees in relation to others. He contrasted life in the kingdom with life under the law. In the section before us now (6:1–18) Jesus shows how righteousness in the kingdom is to surpass the religious practices of the Pharisees in relation to God.

Jesus examined three Jewish modes of worship or piety, and in so doing he contrasted the publicity-seeking piety and worship of the Pharisees with genuine worship in the areas of almsgiving, prayer, and fasting. He exhorted his disciples to give alms in secret, pray in private, and avoid outward signs of fasting.

Many Jewish scholars today object to the unfavorable report given about the Pharisees in the New Testament. They question whether the vices castigated by Jesus were typical of the Pharisees as a whole or were practiced by a small minority. They quickly point out that seven types of Pharisees were mentioned in the Babylonian Talmud (5th century A.D.). Five of these types fit the description of the Pharisees given by Jesus in Matthew 23. The other two were the God-fearing and God-loving Pharisees. In addition to the self-criticism of the Pharisees by Babylonian rabbis, we have further knowledge concerning the divisions among this group of religious teachers. In the first century A.D. the Pharisees were divided into two schools of thought. Some were the followers of Hillel, a more liberal interpreter of the Law who came from Babylonia, while others became the disciples of Shammai, a more conservative scholar. Perhaps Jesus' denunciations were directed more against the disciples of Shammai because they were extremely legalistic.

While the Gospels give more space to the unfavorable side of the Pharisees, an observing reader can discover sayings and incidents in the life of Jesus which clearly indicate that Jesus was not at odds with all of this group. Repeatedly he was invited to dine with Pharisees (Luke 7:36; 11:37; 14:1). The Pharisees were the first to warn Jesus about the plot of Herod Antipas against his life (Luke 13:31). Joseph of Arimathea, the man who made arrangements with Pilate for Jesus' burial, was probably a Pharisee (Mark 15:43; Luke 23:50). In John's Gospel Nicodemus is called a Pharisee (3:1).

The theme of Matthew 6:1–18 is found in verse one. Jesus warned his disciples about practicing their righteousness in order to receive praise and adulation from others. This verse is an introductory remark about the manner in which the three righteous acts in Judaism were to be observed. What applied to the Jews also applies to Christians today. One of the weaknesses of human nature is to do something with a flourish in order to gain the praise and admiration of others.

Giving to Others

Matthew 6:1–4

Almsgiving in Judaism was both a privilege and a primary duty. At the end of every three years the Hebrews were required to store up the tithes of their produce for the benefit of the poor (Deut 14:28–29). In addition, the Deuteronomic law restricted the owner of a field, vineyard, or olive orchard from harvesting all his grain, grapes, and olives so that a portion might be left for the poor, the orphan, the widow, and the alien resident (Deut 24:19–21).

In Ancient Jewish writings not included in the Old Testament, we discover numerous exhortations in behalf of the poor. These writings appeal for help to the needy, but some of them also promised rewards to the donors. They taught that giving alms removed sins, delivered a person from death, and stored up merit toward God. Almsgiving was an established practice in Jesus' day. The Pharisees taught that the religious acts of helping the poor, prayer, and fasting were the chief expressions of true religion. Abundant evidence demonstrates that the Pharisees fully supported these three religious practices. Performance of these spiritual exercises was not dependent on worship in the temple. They could be carried out in any part of the world.

In this section of the Sermon on the Mount, Jesus did not use the antithetical expression, "You have heard that it was said, but I say to you" as he did in Chapter Five. Also he did not say, "If you give alms" but "When you give alms." Thus it was a foregone assumption that the disciples would give to the needy. The early Christian community recognized the importance of giving to the poor and continued this practice. Those who had wealth shared their possessions with the poor, the widows, and orphans (Acts 2:45; 4:34–35; 6:1). Helping those who were in need became a binding factor in the early church. When Agabus, the prophet, announced to the Christians in Syrian Antioch that there would be a famine throughout the world, immediately the church sent a relief fund to the poor saints in Jerusalem (Acts 11:27–30). Paul urged the churches in Achaia and Macedonia to make a contribution for the poor in Jerusalem (Rom 15:26–28; 1 Cor 16:1–4; 2 Cor 8:1–7; 9:1–5). He expected that this expression of generosity by the Gentile Christians would ease the tensions between Jewish and Gentile Christians.

How are we to give to the poor? Certainly not in the way the hypocrites do with fanfare, pomp, and ceremony. We do not display our generosity with the blast of a trumpet. Probably the word trumpet which Jesus used was the *shophar* (ram's horn) rather than a metal instrument. The *shophar* was sounded for various religious and secular events in Jewish life. It was blown for special public fasts and during the time of drought, calling the people to prayer. It seems likely that Jesus used trumpets figuratively. He may not have thought specifically about the Jewish custom, but rather was referring to those who gave alms with a big noise to draw attention to themselves.

The word "hypocrite" is a transliteration of the Greek word that means "play actor." This is a person who dons a mask to play a part. As long as the mask is worn, it is impossible to know the real person behind the mask. The hypocrite pretends that he is someone other than himself. What group did Jesus designate as hypocrites? Did he refer to the Pharisees? Previously we have noted that the rabbis recognized and condemned five kinds of Pharisees who were hypocrites. We have also noted that not all Pharisees were play actors. It is true that

Matthew 23 scathes the Pharisees as hypocrites. It is assumed that Jesus had in mind a certain group of Pharisees who were hypocrites.

The hypocrites made their contributions to those in need in order to exhibit their generosity before people to get their approval and praise. Their motive in giving was wrong. They gave with a flourish and expected to be admired by the spectators for their piety. If they gave for this reason, then they had already received their reward. The Greek word from which we have the translation "received in full" is *apechein*. Ordinarily *apechein* means "to hold back," "keep off," "receive," or "it is enough." In examples from the papyri, however, the verb was used in connection with business transactions, payment of rent, and payment of taxes and bills. In this context *apechein* carried the meaning of a payment in full or the receipt of full payment. Jesus meant that those who gave their money to the needy to curry the favor of others and gain their applause were fully paid. They gave to be praised, and the reward was received by them in full payment. They got the approval of humanity, but they did not get the approval of God.

Secrecy is the magic word in giving alms. In fact, our contributions are to be so secret that the left hand does not know what the right hand is doing. Jesus used this expression to stress secrecy in giving. It is probably a proverb or a wayside saying to illustrate how the relation between the left hand and the right hand typify the closest fellowship imaginable. If this is correct, then Jesus meant that we are not to let our closest friends know about our gifts to the needy. The rabbis condemned those who gave alms in order to be exalted by the spectators, but at the same time they commended those who gave to the poor in secret.

According to the Mishnah (the codification of the oral tradition in the second century A.D.) there was a Chamber of Secrets in the Herodian Temple. The devout Jews placed their gifts in this chamber, and the poor came to this place to receive support in secret. The depository for the poor in the Temple protected the donor from the temptation of seeking approval of people and at the same time relieved the recipient of the embarrassment of accepting charity.

In verse four we learn that God favors our giving in secret, and if we give in this manner, we shall receive a reward. Notice that in the King James Version the adverb "openly" is added to the verb "reward." "Openly" does not occur in the oldest Greek manuscripts of the New Testament. This adverb was probably added by a scribe who felt that the world should know that almsgiving out of love has a visible reward. But if one's motive for giving to the needy secretly is to buy favor with God, he or she is not better than a person who gives publicly to win the applause of other persons.

Giving to the needy should be a primary concern of Christians today. This is part of our ministry. Millions of people in our world need food, clothing, shelter, and medical attention. We should be motivated to relieve the distress of humanity by an unselfish love that goes beyond a sense of duty or the attempt to buy the approval of God or the admiration of people. The reward that we receive is the awareness of having done what God would have us do. When we give our money to help the poor and when we contribute to the church, we ought to consider this action as a happy privilege.

Prayer

Matthew 6:5–8

The Jews had prescribed times for prayer in public worship and private devotions. Formalized prayers were used in worship at the synagogue. At the stated hours of prayer in the Temple (nine in the morning and three in the afternoon), all Jews were expected to pray privately the prescribed prayers or make their own petitions no matter where they were or what they were doing. The set times for prayer in Judaism offered an opportunity for devout persons to participate in wholesome spiritual discipline. They also gave the hypocrites the chance to advance themselves by exhibiting a sham piety. To use one's highest means of communication with God as an occasion for parading piety is the worst kind of hypocrisy. Jesus severely denounced and condemned those who corrupted this practice.

Just as he took it for granted that his disciples would aid the poor with their money, Jesus also assumed that they would pray. He set a noble example for them by practicing this form of worship himself. Matthew did not dwell on the prayer life of Jesus, but one of the characteristics of Luke's Gospel is his presentation of Jesus as a man of prayer. Peculiar to Luke is the description of Jesus praying when he was baptized by John the Baptist (3:21). Luke also indicates that Jesus prayed all night before he selected his twelve disciples (6:12). Also after praying, Jesus asked his disciples what they and others believed about his person and mission (9:18). Luke notes it was while Jesus was praying that he was transfigured (9:29). Luke records that after observing Jesus pray, one disciple requested him to teach all the disciples to pray (11:1).

The parading of one's special sanctity before people destroys the spirit of prayer just as the ostentatious display of one's generosity kills the spirit of giving. While the congregation was gathered in the synagogues for sabbath worship or at the set times for prayer, the hypocrites displayed their dedication to God in order that they might receive the admiration of the assembly. They probably did not recite the daily prayers with the other worshipers but uttered their own private petitions. They were using prayer to play to the galleries.

A more conspicuous place for a person to exhibit devotion to religious duties was in a public thoroughfare or the marketplace. On days of public fasts or when there was a drought, the Jews had a service in the streets or marketplaces. The leaders gathered around the ark containing the Law, and after an address by a rabbi, they called the people to genuine repentance. We are not to suppose that the hypocrites deliberately went to the street corners to pray. They were more subtle than that. They probably planned to be in a public place at the fixed time for prayers so that they could show off their devotion. The street corners, where business was transacted, assured the hypocrite of a large audience. If a person prays strictly for the purpose of collecting admirers of his piety and gets his fans, then full payment is given for his efforts. The hypocrite gets what he or she sought. It is praise from people, and disapproval from God.

Instead of publicly displaying our piety through prayer, Jesus exhorts us to withdraw from public eyes and pray in secret. "Go into your room, close the door and pray to your father" (v. 6). The word in Greek that is translated "room" originally meant "a store chamber." Later it referred to privacy in general. It is understood as a figure of complete privacy here, as it is in Luke 12:3 and Matthew 24:26. When we pray, we are to withdraw into the secrecy of our inner selves and close the door, whether literally or figuratively, against the disturbing and distracting thoughts that seize us. In private we are stripped of our disguises and are open to God. We have no audience to hear us and no one to applaud our righteousness.

The reward of true and sincere prayer is not named. Genuine prayer carries its own reward. In genuine prayer a person exposes the inner self completely to God in earnest simplicity and communes with him. Fellowship with God is our reward. We must hasten to say that Jesus did not denounce public prayer. When he went to worship service in the synagogue, he participated in public prayer. In Acts we notice that the early church engaged in public prayer without any sense of disobeying a teaching of Jesus.

Jesus warned against putting on a show with our praying like the hypocrites, but he also cautioned against praying like the pagans. Verse seven says, "Do not keep on babbling like pagans." The Greek word translated here "babbling" is very rare. The etymology of *battalogein* is disputed, but its meaning is understood to be "repetition of words," "chatter," "heap up empty phrases," and "babbling." The prayers of the pagans were senseless chatter or babblings to get the attention of the gods. Their petitions were nothing more than incantations designed to act like a charm on the gods or to make them do what the worshiper wanted. More than one philosopher of ancient times said that the prayers of the people were so long that they made the gods weary.

Jesus did not condemn the length of time spent in prayer or sincere repetition in prayer by this criticism of the pagans. He spent long hours in prayer, and in Gethsemane he prayed three times for the removal of suffering on the cross (Matt 26:39, 42,

44). Jesus denounced pagan babbling because it sought to goad the deity into action.

In verse eight Jesus tells us that God does not have to be informed of our needs as though he was out of touch with life. This sort of prayer downgrades the character of God. It is a reflection on his knowledge. Even before we pray God is already concerned for our welfare. In our praying we should not try to make God conform to our wishes, but we should conform to the will of God. When we make our petitions known to God, we do so on the assumption that we have real knowledge about God's ways and thoughts. What we know of God comes to us through Scripture and through God's revelation in Jesus Christ. It is for this reason that we call on God through the name of Christ. Christ's name stands for his character. Through his character we know what God is like. Sometimes it is frightening, indeed, when we close our prayers in the name of Christ. It is frightening simply because we are not certain that our petitions are consistent with the character of God revealed in Christ.

The Disciple's Prayer

Matthew 6:9–13

After Jesus instructed his listeners concerning how they were not to pray, he set forth a positive pattern for prayer. This prayer we know as the Lord's Prayer or the Disciples' Prayer. Though the prayer is absent from Mark, our earliest Gospel, there is no doubt that Jesus presented this model to his disciples. Matthew and Luke introduced it at different points in their respective records and with considerable textual variations. In

Matthew's Gospel, the prayer forms part of the Sermon on the Mount; its simplicity is contrasted with the "empty phrases" and "many words" in which not only the pagans but the Jews habitually indulged. Luke, on the other hand, supplies a different setting. He inserts the prayer in his travel narrative immediately after Jesus' visit to the home of Mary and Martha. Luke tells us quite definitely that the request for a form of prayer was addressed to Jesus by one of his disciples when "he was praying in a certain place" (Luke 11:1).

Luke's version of the prayer is shorter and simpler than Matthew's account, and many scholars believe that it is closer to the original form. The abrupt address "*Abba*" (Father) in Luke becomes in Matthew "Our Father who is in heaven," a liturgical form. Matthew also has two additional petitions, "Your will be done" and "deliver us from evil."

Much has been written to prove the Lord's Prayer was either dependent or independent of Jewish sources. It is quite evident from both Matthew's and Luke's version that some phrases in the prayer have parallels in the old Jewish liturgical prayers. Most certainly the people in Palestine prayed fervently for the coming of God's rule. They also prayed for the consecration of God's name. Thousands from humble homes in Galilee and Judea must have made petitions to God for daily food. The originality of Jesus in the presentation of the model prayer lies in his approach to God and his selection and combination of petitions. The form which he produced bears the mark of his unique character. It rests on the assurance that God is Father of all humanity, that God's will is best, and that God knows all who pray and hears each one.

The Lord's Prayer begins with an address to God. How are we to think of God? How are we to relate to God? What is

God's attitude toward us? All of these questions are answered in the use of the designation of "Father" for God and the use of the first personal plural pronouns "our," "we," and "us" which rules out our individual desires and places them in the sphere of community concern. Jesus did not invent the term Father in relation to God. It was used in the Old Testament and in the Apocrypha, but he most assuredly did give it a new meaning and prominence.

Jesus was far more concerned that people come to know God as Father than that they meet the legal and ritual requirements of the religious establishment. To be sure the address of the prayer is to God, the Father, who is in heaven indicating that God is transcendent. His thoughts are not our thoughts. God's ways are not our ways. While God is lifted above us, God is with us, and God desires that all accept God's thoughts and follow in God's way. The prayers of Jesus indicate his sense of the immediate presence of God as he prayed. Until this filial relationship is recognized by us, we can hardly pray according to the pattern of prayer that Jesus gave us. All other concerns are secondary to a right relationship with God.

The first three petitions of the Lord's Prayer extol the majesty, sovereignty, and greatness of god. The verbs are in the imperative mode to indicate commanding assertions. They could possibly be hortatory, but they are certainly not imperatives in the sense of entreaties as are the final four petitions. As commanding assertions we should translate the first three petitions in this manner: "Your name is to be consecrated," "your rule is to come," and "Your will is to be accomplished."

The first petition of the prayer is "Your name is to be consecrated." God's name stands for God's character and beneficent purpose for humankind and the world. The Old Testa-

Testament writers often declared that "the fear of the Lord is the beginning of wisdom." They recognized that respect and reverence for God was foundational to any valid relationship with God. God created the world. God sustains it and seeks to bring all things into harmony with God's redemptive purpose. Too often there are those who subordinate the character of God to their own whims, desires, and wants. In doing this they degrade God's character. True reverence for God's name is expressed in our way of life as well as in our worship. Reverence causes us to take God seriously in every area of life.

The second petition is "Your rule is to come." It is a commanding assertion that all people may recognize God's sovereignty and submit to God's rule. No self-centered will or desire can maintain its way in God's presence. When we pray for the rule of God to come, we demonstrate our concern for all those who have not submitted to the sovereignty of God.

The third petition is "Your will is to be accomplished." This petition is equivalent to the preceding one. This may be the reason why Luke omitted it. We are to bend our wills until they are brought into conformity to God's will. Submission to God's rule is an indication that we shall follow God's will.

God's character is to be revered, God's rule is to come, and God's will is to be accomplished on earth as all of these fully exist in the heavens above. This is not a petition to call us to heaven but rather to bring heaven to earth.

From the three petitions which are recognitions of God's honor and sovereignty, the prayer moves on to the disciples' need for daily sustenance. The entreaty, "Give us this day our daily bread," puts human desires under a strong restraint. The natural inclination of people is to ask God for all they want, but when they revere God's name and submit to God's will, they realize that they have no right to request anything more than sufficient provisions to perform their tasks. They must live their lives in daily dependence upon God.

The fifth entreaty in the Lord's Prayer says, "Forgive us our debts, as we also have forgiven our debtors" (6:12). Luke's version of the prayer has "sins" in place of "debts" (11:4). The use of debts as a metaphor for sin was not uncommon in the teachings of Jesus (Matt 18:23–35; Luke 7:41–43). The only petition in the Lord's Prayer which touches upon our relations to others is the one about forgiving. This may come as a surprise to us when we consider the character of Jesus' teachings. Yet when correctly considered, this one petition includes all of our relationships with people. This is the real test of our attitude toward others. A person may be friendly, kind, and generous, but when he or she suffers wrong or injury, is forgiveness a possibility? Only when one is able to forgive can that person be sure that the genuine spirit of love is within.

Jesus considered forgiveness so important in the prayer that he gave a further comment on the subject (6:14–15) when he concluded the prayer. The comment is self explanatory. A person can ask forgiveness only if there is a willingness to forgive. We should not interpret this as arbitrary action of God, but see it as an action which springs from the nature of our relationship with God. Does that mean God's forgiveness is conditional? Does God forgive only as we forgive others? The answer is both yes and no. God's disposition to forgive is not limited to our forgiveness. An unforgiving spirit, however, shuts out God's forgiveness even when God is willing to forgive. A person is not ready to be forgiven as long as there is no willingness to forgive. The problem is not that God is reluctant to forgive us, but rather that our obstinate and rebellious spirit refuses to enter into the fullness of forgiveness. Praying for forgiveness should prompt a person to forgive. (See the Parable of the Unmerciful Servant in Matthew 18:15–35).

The sixth and seventh entreaties we shall combine into one because they both have to do with a plea for aid against sin. Luke has "lead us not into temptation" but does not include "deliver from evil (or the evil one)." The petition "lead us not into temptation" has caused considerable difficulty to thoughtful Christians. In the English language "temptation" means generally an enticement to sin. But does God induce people to sin? Elsewhere we read, "no one being tempted is to say, 'I am tempted by God'; for God is not tempted with evil and he himself tempts no one; but each one is tempted while being lured and enticed by his own desires." (Jas 1:13–14).

The Greek substantive *peirasmos* in the Lord's Prayer has a dual meaning. It conveys the notion of enticement to do *evil* or *good* as well as testing. James is aware of this twofold meaning of the word. The inducement to do evil is clearly understood by him in the reference above where he uses his substantive *peirasmos*, the verbal adjective *apeirastos* with the alpha privitive to mean "untempted," and the verb *peirazō*. In another place, however, he uses the substantive *peirasmos* to indicate "trials" or "tests."

Perhaps a better translation of the sixth petition would be "lead us not into trials," since temptation is generally understood as an enticement to sin. Jesus was put on trial by the devil in the desert before he began his ministry. He faced another test after feeding the five thousand. The Galileans tried to force him to become king (John 6:15). In the Garden of Gethsemane on the eve of the crucifixion Jesus was put to the test again when he prayed, "My father, if it is possible, let this cup pass from me; nevertheless not as I will but as you will." (Matt 26:39 and parallels).

God does permit the testing of a person's fidelity, but God does not entice us. Every testing involves a calculated risk. There is always the possibility that people might give in to sin. The nature of our plea is then a cry for help. We are afraid that we cannot pass the test, and we anxiously desire to be delivered from the evil that besets us. We can, however, depend upon God, who will not let us face a trial beyond our strength, and with the test there is always a way of deliverance (1 Cor 10:13).

In the Revised Standard Version and in some other translations the doxology of the Lord's Prayer is noticeably absent. The familiar line, "For yours is the kingdom and the power and the glory, for ever, Amen," does not appear in the most reliable manuscripts. The Didache, a Christian document on Church Order, gives the Lord's Prayer with essentially the same wording and adds the doxology. Scholars are not in agreement with respect to the dating, ranging from the last decade of the first century A.D. to the end of the second century. It is quite clear from the Didache, however, that the Lord's Prayer was put to liturgical use in the church, and this may explain the addition of the doxology here and in some manuscripts. It is possible that the early church constructed the doxology after the pattern of the doxology in 1 Chronicles 29:11.

Fasting

Matthew 6:16–18

The Mosaic law did not contain a requirement for fasting. Later, the rabbis understood Leviticus 16:31, "You must deny yourselves," to mean that people should fast on the Day of Atonement. This was the only prescribed fast in Judaism. Though the Jews did abstain from food in the observance of days commemorating calamities in Jewish history and during declared public fasts, they were not required by law to do this. In addition to the annual fast on the Day of Atonement prescribed for all, the Pharisees fasted on Mondays and Thursdays of each week. They selected these days because they believed that Moses ascended Mount Sinai on Monday to receive the law from God and descended on Thursday. Jesus was criticized because his disciples did not follow the Pharisees' calendar on fasting (Matt 9:14). Jesus did fast (4:2), but his fasting was reserved for times of sorrow or during a crisis rather than a scheduled time like that of the Pharisees.

The purpose of fasting in Judaism was to express sorrow for the death of a person or for national disaster, to call the people to national repentance, to show that an individual's penitence was genuine, to practice the presence of God, to fulfill a vow, or to get God's attention. The hypocrites who were reprimanded by Jesus were taking advantage of private fasts to gain a reputation for exemplary righteousness by the people who watched them.

Fasting, as the Jews practiced it, is not a usual part of our Christian tradition. Some abstain from food in order to decrease their weight. Others fast so they can understand the feelings of those who are starving and, at the same time, appreciate the food they have. A few abstain from food, water, and sleep because of inner feelings of sorrow and a sense of deep repentance.

The hypocrites advertised that they were fasting by looking dismal and having a sullen or gloomy countenance. They thought this kind of appearance was in keeping with the practice of the religious exercise of fasting. The hypocrites disfigured their faces so that people could detect that they were fasting. In verse 18b there is a play on words in the Greek text. The hypocrites make their faces "disappear" in order to make them "appear" to men as fasting. They put on theatrical makeup like actors in a play. They let their faces disappear under a deposit of dirt and ashes to make themselves appear to have a sanctimonious look. The fasts of the Pharisees became a stage on which they could parade their holiness. By their ostentatious display of piety, the hypocrites caused this act of worship to degenerate from an act of faith into a shadow of fashion.

Jesus assumed that his disciples would fast, but he did not want them to advertise their fasting by external signs, like putting ashes on their heads and scattering dirt on their bodies. The disciples were to appear in public with a look of joy, not sorrow. Putting oil on the head was a symbol of cleanliness, the opposite of dirt and ashes. By removing the makeup that shows the public a person is fasting, the approval now is not from an admiring public but from God. God will see what is done in secret and will reward the worshiper for his or her sincerity.

True righteousness comes from within a person. It issues from an inner life that has been transformed by the power of God in Christ. Genuine righteousness displays mercy, justice, love, and faithfulness in all of life's relationships. Its outward display is consistent with inner character. Outward conduct is all of a piece with what we are in ourselves. In our fellowship with God we are sincere, humble, and intent on what is pure, holy, good, and just. When we come into contact with society, we continue to be what we are in the presence of God.

Questions for Reflection

1. What kind of person is a hypocrite?

2. In what manner should a person give to the poor?

3. What is the reward for genuine prayer?

4. Jesus warned us to avoid praying like the pagans. What was the nature of pagan prayers?

5. Did Jesus annul public prayer?

6. What is the essence of the first three petitions in the Lord's prayer?

7. What is the focus of the last four petitions of the prayer?

8. At the conclusion of the Lord's prayer Matthew gives a more detailed statement with respect to one of the petitions. What is this petition?

9. How do you explain the petition "lead us not into temptation" that is contained in the Lord's prayer?

10. Was the doxology in the Lord's prayer originally a part of the prayer?

11. What was the purpose of fasting in Judaism? Should we fast today? If so, for what purpose?

Chapter 4

POSSESSIONS AND ANXIETY

Matthew 6:19–34

Previously in the Sermon on the Mount we noted how the righteousness of Jesus' followers is to exceed the kind of righteousness practiced by the Pharisees and scribes in human relationships (5:19–48). We further perceived that the disciples of Jesus are to exceed the righteousness of the Pharisees and scribes in acts of worship (6:18). In Matthew 6:19–7:12 Jesus turned the spotlight on two continuing human problems. They are possessions and anxiety.

Possessions

Matthew 6:19–21

The first problem that Jesus introduced was possessions or treasures. He cautioned his disciples against accumulating and hoarding worldly goods as their ground of security. Jesus was not opposed to accumulating property or storing up for future needs. He did, however, warn against the use of these as an end and goal of life rather than a means toward an end. On one occasion he said, "A man's life does not consist in the abundance of possessions" (Luke 12:15).

Many people of the first century A.D. in Galilee had few possessions. Whatever they did own, they held on to for dear life. They may have possessed valuable garments, a few metal ornaments, grain for food, and some coins. Their poverty did not prevent them from desiring the finer things possessed by the rich. But Jesus cautioned them, as he does us, about earthly treasures being under multiple threats of perishability or loss.

If a person's treasure consisted in clothing, there was always the attendant enemy. It was the consuming insect, the moth. The moth can riddle a piece of cloth in short order and render the possession valueless. Another enemy that Jesus mentioned was rust. "Rust" is the translation of the Greek word *brōsis*. *Brōsis* literally means "eaten away." This word has the meaning of rust when used in a metaphorical sense. If Jesus meant rust, he had in mind those whose treasure was precious metals. People in those days would bury their precious metals in the ground to avoid having them stolen. But Jesus reminded them that they had overlooked the danger of rust, which could destroy metals.

If another common meaning of *brōsis* was Jesus' intent, the reference is to the manner in which rats and worms can consume grain that is stored in a granary. Rats and worms would not only eat the grain but pollute it as well. In addition to the moth, rust, or rats and worms, Jesus introduced a third enemy to possession. This enemy is a thief. The word for "break in" actually means "dig through" in the Greek text. In Palestine the walls of most houses were made of clay (somewhat like adobe), and a burglar could enter a house by digging through the wall.

The picture here is that of a man who thought that his house guaranteed security for his treasures. He did not take into consideration the cleverness of a smart thief. Those who cautiously hide their treasures in their houses must not foolishly ignore the possibility of a burglar's digging through and stealing their possessions. With the increasing number of people burglarized today, we are keenly aware of this threat to our cherished possessions.

In addition to natural deterioration and theft, death always poses an imminent danger of separating us from our treasures. Jesus clearly portrayed this threat in his parable of the rich fool (Luke 12:16–21). Against the inevitability of death and the issues of afterlife, the person of property is as bare and defenseless as the destitute.

Today Jesus might not talk about fabrics, precious metals, or other such treasures admired by Galilean peasants. Perhaps he would say something about money, land investments, credit ratings, insurance policies, stocks and bonds, savings accounts, and other securities. These also have their attendant enemies in fluctuation of the stock market, inflation, depression, and war.

Rather than store up treasures on earth Jesus urged his listeners to store up treasures in heaven (v. 20). The genuine treasures of life are not found in material possessions, which are perishable, but in spiritual values that lie beyond the ravages of time, theft, and death. The secular world ascribes ultimate value to transitory material things. Jesus calls us to focus on our attention on moral and spiritual values that are permanent.

Matthew did not specify what these treasures in heaven are or how they may be obtained. In a similar passage Luke indicated that these treasures come by giving to the poor (12:33). In his letter to the Colossians, the apostle Paul gave some light on the matter. He said, "If then you have been raised with Christ, seek the things that are above, not on things that are on the earth" (3:1–2). Clearly from verses 12–17 of the same chapter, we comprehend what Paul means by "things that are above." He spoke of compassion, meekness, patience, peace, love, forgiveness, and forbearance. Spiritual values are moth-proof, rustproof, worm and rat resistant, burglar proof, and death defiant. Earthly treasures depreciate in value, but heavenly treasures appreciate in value. Material values are transient and temporal, but spiritual values are lasting and eternal.

Jesus warned, "Where your treasure is, there your heart will be also" (v. 21). The treasure a person selects in life is inextricably tied up with the heart. The word "heart" in Jesus' day meant more than it does to us today. The heart represented one's total self. It was the person's whole life. Whatever we choose as the highest good becomes our treasure. This treasure in turn is tied up with our life. If something can destroy or remove the treasure, our life will collapse. Can a change in the political structure, a loss of health, some new scientific discovery, or some economic change sweep away my treasure? If so, I have the wrong treasure, and the preservation of my whole personhood is in danger.

Serving One Master

Matthew 6:22–24

After verse 19–21 Matthew inserted a statement of Jesus in parabolic form. It illustrates the necessity for spiritual insight in order to discern the true values of life. The eye, which is the lamp of the body, must be sound and in proper focus; otherwise, a person blinds himself or herself to the treasures of heaven. The eye is considered here to be the window of the body. The condition of the window determines the amount of light that shines into a room. If the window is clean, light will illuminate the whole room. But if the window is dirty, light is obstructed, and the room is bound to remain in darkness. In a moral sense the spiritual state of the eye determines the character of the individual.

Jesus said, "So, if your eye is *single* . . ." (v. 22b). Scholars vary in their translation of the Greek word *haplous* ("single"). The New International Version has "good." The King James Version translates *haplous* with the word "single" while the Revised Standard Version has "sound." Others insist that *haplous* in this verse has the meaning of "generous." The literal meaning of the word in Greek is "single"; and if verse 22–23 are directly connected to verse 24, it would seem that Matthew has "single" in mind.

If a person possesses a single eye, his or her vision is clear, sound, and free from distortions (double vision or blurring). The spiritual eye that directs its line of vision toward God sees the true value of things. Singleness of devotion to God opens the way for the fullness of God's light.

In contrast to the eyes fully focused on God to remove distortions, Jesus set forth the possibility of the eyes being bad, evil, or not sound. When our vision is darkened by prejudice, hate, lust, jealousy, self-conceit, and conflicting goals, we cannot see things clearly. These distortions can prevent us from seeing the light of the knowledge of God in Christ. The parallel of this in Luke's Gospel has, "Therefore be careful lest the light in you be darkness" (11:35). If our lives are illuminated by divine truth, we will have the light of life and avoid darkness.

Jesus further warned, "No one can serve two masters" (v. 24). Possibly a better translation would be "No one can be a slave to two owners." In the slavery system of the first century A.D., two men could not own the same slave. The owner had life and death control over the slave. He could not allow his slave to give allegiance to any other person. He demanded supreme loyalty from him or her. In our relationship to God, homage cannot be divided. God demands exclusive service from us just as the owner of a slave had complete authority over the life and time of his slave.

Most translators have used "mammon" instead of "money" in verse 24b. "Mammon" (more appropriately *mamōn*) is a translation of a Semitic word that means "material possession." It was not always used in a bad sense. *Mamōn* was property or money a person entrusted to someone to keep safe for him. Later the word changed in meaning from an entrustment to something in which a person placed complete trust. Thus material possessions became equivalent to a god. *Mamōn* is personified in this verse as a rival to God.

Jesus did not condemn wealth, but he did condemn our enslavement to riches. Wealth is a trust, but it is not something in which we place our trust. Possessions are instruments to be used, but they are not to be used for selfish enjoyment. Rather, they are to be used for the good of others and ourselves. The chief end or goal of Christians is to love God supremely and give God our best service. It is impossible to do this if material possessions become the chief concern in life.

The true measure of life is not found in that by which we live but in that for which we live. We live *by* our possessions that we accumulate, but we live *for* those things money cannot buy. We live *by* the hour, the day, the week, and the year, but we live *for* eternity. We live by the commonplace experiences in life, but we live *for* extraordinary spiritual experience with God.

Anxiety

Matthew 6:25–30

Jesus in 6:25–34 goes far beyond the teaching in 6:24. He warned his disciples not only to avoid serving riches as a god but also to rid themselves of anxious concern about the ordinary needs of life. The connective "therefore" in verse 25 seems to be used in a very loose sense. After verse 24 we would expect a conclusion something like this, "Therefore serve God and renounce wealth." The "therefore" must refer to an assurance of God's care for those who trust him. It is clear from Luke's Gospel that Jesus meant to draw a conclusion from the parable of the rich fool (12:22).

Five times in this section of the Sermon on the Mount the Greek word *merimnan* appears (vv. 25,27,28,31,34). The translation "do no worry" is better than "take no thought" (KJV). William Tyndale, prior to the King James Version, translated *merimnan* with the negative as "be not careful." "Careful" for Tyndale was "full of care." Possibly a better translation is "do not be overly anxious" or "do not be distracted."

The warnings of Jesus to his followers about over-anxiety concerning life refers not just to life of the spirit but to natural life. It is the kind of life that is preserved by food and drink and kept comfortable by clothing. Jesus did use both life and body, but he did not refer to them as separate entities as the Greeks did. The Greeks looked upon the body as a prison of the soul. The Hebrews taught that the person was a single unit. Life is the self, and the body is an essential part, so it also is the self. Both life and body comprise the self, the character of the person over against temporal food and clothing.

Jesus accepted the Hebrew concept of a person as a total entity. He realized that the continuation of life was dependent on nourishment, and the protection of the body as dependent on clothing. He cautioned his disciples, however, about becoming distracted by these necessities of life.

To teach trust in God's providential care and the folly of over-anxiety about bodily needs for the future, Jesus set forth one of the principles of interpretation introduced by a rabbi of the first century A.D. This *Qal Wahomer* principle, as it was called, argued from light to heavy or heavy to light, or as we would say, from minor to major or major to minor. In a more argumentative form it would be something like this, "If God has given life—which is more important than food, drink and clothing—will God not give the lesser gifts to sustain life?"

If God gives the great gift of life, God will supply temporal needs. God's interest in us does not cease after giving us life and body. We are to trust God for food, drink, and clothing as we trust God for life and body. We are the children of God, and God still loves us and cares for us. If a Christian becomes overly anxious about the necessities of life, it reflects distrust of God. Faith says that God will provide whatever is essential to sustain life. Food, drink, and clothing function to enrich life, not to become distractions.

Job was challenged to look at nature to understand the nature of God (chaps. 38–41). In like manner Jesus directed the attention of his followers to God's providential care of birds, flowers, and grass. The birds do not plant a crop. Since they do not sow, there is nothing for them to harvest and store for future use. Note that they are not commended for idleness but for freedom from corroding care and over-anxiety. The birds work for a living, searching for worms and insects. They also diligently build their nests. But the birds are carefree and happy. They are not troubled about the supply of worms and insects. They do not wear themselves out providing for future needs. Every now and then, after downing an insect or pulling up a worm and building a nest, the birds will sing a song. If God cares for these creatures, why would God not care for us.

In the Lord's Prayer, Jesus included daily bread as one of the requests (Matt 6:11; Luke 11:3). The petition is only for bread for one day at a time. Worried fear about not having an abundance of food for the future takes the joy out of life. Being distracted by storing up provisions for the future can be a subtle form of worship of *mamōn*. One can begin with prudent foresight, but in the end make food and clothes a tyrannical god.

The apostle Paul, in his letter to the Philippians, put it this way:

> Not that I complain of want; for I have learned, in whatever state I am, to be content. I know how to be abased, and I know how to abound; in any and all circumstances I have learned the secret of facing plenty and hunger, abundance and want (4:11–12).

In verse 27 the Greek word *pēchys*, which is sometimes translated "hour," is really a measurement of 18 inches. It is a measurement of space not time. The Greek word behind the translation "life" in this verse is *hēlikia*, which can mean age, stature, or duration of life. If we take *pēchys* to mean "a cubit or 18 inches" and *hēlikia* to mean "stature," Jesus would be saying that a person cannot through over-anxiety increase his or her height by 18 inches. Yet who is going to be overly concerned about adding this huge amount of growth unless the person wishes to be a basketball player. It seems better to take *hēlikia* to mean duration of life or age. But what are we to do about *pēchys*, which is a spacial not a temporal measurement? In Psalm 39:5 a space measurement is used as a temporal standard, "You have made my days a mere handbreadth." The handbreadth was a measure of about three inches. Thus Jesus is saying the corroding care cannot lengthen life. On the contrary, the pressures of life might contribute to shortening life. In Luke's Gospel (12:20) it was the prolongation of life that the rich fool failed to secure.

Following the teaching of God's care for us in the matter of food, Jesus directed the attention of his listeners to another illustration from nature—the flowers that burst forth in Galilee in the springtime. Just as birds are not distracted by anxiety about food, so the lilies of the field have no fretful concern about being clothed. The lilies of the field are not what we would normally call lilies. Even today the Arabs in Palestine call a number of wild flowers lilies. What Jesus referred to were probably anemones that adorn the hillsides of Palestine in spring. These anemones have a beauty of their own. Yet they do not busy themselves with spinning and toiling to produce a beauty unmatched by human artistry. God is the one who provides this beauty.

Solomon was a classic example of wealth among the Jews (1 Kings 10:4–7). He wore gorgeous clothes, and if he had been around in modern times, he would have been declared the best-dressed man of the year. All of his finery, however, could not match the beauty of flowers. God excels all in his expression of beauty in nature. Some scholars take the grass mentioned in verse 30 to mean the flowers that have died. They say that Jesus wished to stress the transiency of the beauty of flowers and to contrast this with humanity. Others believe that Jesus replaced the wild flowers with wild grass as a figure of speech. The latter seems to be more appropriate because dead grass would more likely be used for fuel than would dead flowers. Today the grass is green, but tomorrow it is dead and fit only to be used for fuel. If God is so extravagant in showing care of the grass that is short–lived, how much more will God love and care for us. Those who do not trust God to provide clothes and food for the body have little faith. Faith makes a person aware of his or her dependence on God. Compulsive worry is a vote of no confidence in God and a lack of faith in ourselves.

Jesus reminded them that "The pagans seek all these things" (v. 31). The pagans believed in unpredictable and cruel gods who were fickle and responded to their worshipers according to their whims and capricious ideas. Our God responds to worshipers with love and immeasurable mercy. We never catch our God at a time when God is emotionally disturbed. God is always concerned for us and knows that we need the necessities of life.

The Greatest Treasure

Matthew 6:31–34

If food, drink, and clothing are not to have priority, what does? In verses 31–34 Jesus tells us that the center of life is God's rule and righteousness. People cannot divest themselves of all anxiety, but if their quest is the kingdom righteousness, they can lower their anxiety level. Matthew summed up this section (verses 31–34) of Jesus' teaching with the demand of Jesus for us to seek the sovereignty of God over our lives and come into a right relationship with God. A follower must unconditionally surrender to the will of God. Over-anxiety about things gets in the way of the rule of God.

We note that the exact wording of many of the ancient manuscripts varies slightly but retains a common character. Some have "kingdom of God and his righteousness" while others have "the kingdom and righteousness of God." Still others have "his righteousness and kingdom." In all of these alterations both "kingdom" and "righteousness" have been retained. In our study of Matthew's Gospel thus far, we have noticed that this emphasis on the kingdom and righteousness is a characteristic of this Gospel.

Perhaps one might wonder if he or she could survive by putting God's sovereignty and righteousness first. To calm our fears, Jesus said that God would provide what we need. He does not suggest that those who seek God's will are obligated to go hungry or naked. Nor does he encourage laziness. The promise is contingent on accepting God's rule and righteousness first.

Some scholars suggest that verse 34 comes as an anticlimax after verse 33. While it is true that the ending of the section at verse 33 seems appropriate, verse 34 is highly important and has a direct bearing on the discussion of corroding care. Jesus said that it is foolish to add the burdensome cares of tomorrow to the cares of today. All we are doing is increasing the over–concerns of today without making those of tomorrow any lighter. Remember that "do not worry" is the same expression used in verse 25. The warning is against being overly anxious or becoming distracted about what is happening in the future. There is no reason for us to double our cares by anticipating them. Each day has its own concerns. We are to live one day at a time. The trouble of today is sufficient. We are to let the troubles of tomorrow come in their own time.

In verses 25–34 Jesus gave seven arguments against over-anxiety. (1) God gives us life and body, so we can trust him to sustain and clothe us. (2) Birds are not overly anxious about their lives. They do not store up for the future, yet they are fed. (3) Worry is useless because it does not prolong life. (4) God clothes the flowers and grass, both of which are transient. (5) Over anxiety is a characteristic of the pagans. (6) Worry can be defeated by a right relationship with God and by allowing God to be the dominating power in our lives. (7) Live one day at a time and stop worrying about tomorrow.

Questions for Reflection

1. What are the two continuing problems for humanity?

2. Why is it so important to be careful about what we select as our ultimate treasure in life?

3. What were three enemies to treasures of the people in Jesus' day?

4. List some of the enemies to the treasures we possess today?

5. What is the essence of the treasures Jesus would have us preserve?

6. What did Jesus mean by the eye being single?

7. Did Jesus condemn wealth?

8. What are the seven arguments that Jesus used against our being overly anxious?

Chapter 5

MISCELLANEOUS TEACHINGS OF THE SERMON

Matthew 7:1–29

In chapter seven of the Sermon on the Mount the author does not display here the same skill of movement in his presentation of the teachings of Jesus as he did in chapters five and six. Heretofore he has managed to show some sort of interconnectedness in the topics which he chose. The chapter begins with a warning about judging and profaning the holy and continues with teachings concerning persistence in prayer, the so-called Golden Rule, the two ways, the two forms of deception, and ends with the parable of the two builders.

On Judging

Matthew 7:1–5

The teaching on judging occurs also in Luke's Gospel (6:37–42). It is found in the Sermon on the Plain and is longer, more poetic, and more illustrative than the sayings in Matthew's Gospel. Furthermore, Luke has placed the instruction on judging immediately after Jesus' appeal to his disciples to love their enemies. In addition to the imperative "judge not" in Matthew, Luke adds three more imperatives: "do not condemn," "forgive," and "give."

Many of the sayings of Jesus are *portable*. By portable I mean that they are easily memorized, and we can carry them in our minds with all ease. At the opportune time we can quote what Jesus said either for a good cause or an evil purpose. There is an advantage to this and also a disadvantage. The portable sayings are advantageous in that we do remember something that Jesus said. But the disadvantage comes when we tend to strip the sayings of their context and, thereby, give a meaning not found in the saying. With respect to judging Jesus said, "Don't go on judging, in order that you may not be judged. For with what judgement you judge you will be judged, and the measure you give will be the measure you get" (7:1–2). For some this is too much to remember, and to accommodate their brain cells they shorten it to the imperative "judge not!" Thus, when someone is quite capable of giving a critical evaluation of a person, an event, or an institution, there will be those who, in a super pious manner, will say, "You know what the Scripture says, 'Judge not!'"

To say that we are not to judge means that Jesus set us a bad example because he was constantly condemning the Pharisees. How can we keep from judging? Why should we not judge? How are we to tell the difference between right and wrong, good and evil, the truth and a lie, if we are unable to make a discrimination between the two? It is quite obvious from the context that this is not the kind of judgment Jesus had in mind. Later on in this chapter Jesus warns his disciples about being taken in and misled by false prophets. He gives us the criterion for forming an opinion (vv. 15–16). It is by their fruits that they are singled out.

Jesus reminded his disciples that the criterion which they used in judging would be used against them by others. Like begets like. A person gets what he or she gives. To reinforce his statement Jesus added, “And the measure you give will be the measure you get” (v. 2b). This same saying is found in the Mishnah, but it bears no relevance to the issues under discussion there (*Mishna Sotah* 1:7).

In verses 3–5 we are introduced to the sort of judgment that Jesus was warning his disciples against. It is a one-sided judgment of one’s brother. The brother has a tiny particle in his eye, and under the guise of helpfulness you want to remove the particle. Jesus questions whether this is help or destruction. How can one see to remove the speck when he is blind? In contrast to the speck in the brother’s eye there is a log jam in your eyes. To be sure, we are blinded by jealousy, fear, outward appearances, gossip, and our own self-righteousness, and as opthalmologists we face a charge of malpractice. It is only as we remove those blind spots from our eyes that we can see clearly to do some good. If not, then our intention is not to help a person but to do harm.

Profaning the Holy
Matthew 7:6

The warning about giving holy things to dogs and throwing pearls before swine appears to be out of kilter with the teachings and deeds of Jesus. This verse does not occur in any of the other Gospels. The Jews classified dogs as scavengers, and they were prohibited from eating hogs because they were unclean. In I Enoch 89:42 the enemies of Israel are called dogs, foxes, and wild boars. On the basis of this extreme hatred for the Gentiles found in certain Jewish apocalyptic works, some consider

Matthew 7:6 as "a bit of apocalyptic Jewish exclusiveness, adopted by extreme Jewish Christians, and incorporated among the sayings of Jesus."[1] his teaching has also been considered as a directive for the primitive church to restrict holy things for holy people. In the *Didache* the Eucharist was restricted to those who had undergone baptism (9:5). There are some who question whether Jesus said this. A few scholars think that the saying has some connection with the pericope about the Syrophoenician woman in Matthew 15:21–28 and Mark 7:24–30. Probably a more accurate interpretation of the verse is that it is a symbolic caveat by Jesus to safeguard his disciples against unnecessary exposure of their precious spiritual teachings to those who could not appreciate them.

Persistence in Prayer

Matthew 7:7–11

Matthew returns to Jesus' teaching on prayer in a loosely added exhortation. Luke places the same material in his Gospel immediately following the parable of the friend at midnight (11:5–7). Jesus gave this parable to instruct his disciples to be persistent in prayer. We also observe that the parable is preceded by the Lord's Prayer. Thus Luke has connected the Lord's Prayer with a teaching on persistence in prayer, while Matthew has separated the two in the Sermon on the Mount.

From Luke's parable and Jesus' comment on the parable in verses 9–10, people might get the notion that God is reluctant to answer their prayers unless they pester God. Did Jesus intend for us to understand that if we apply enough pressure on God, God will answer our prayers because this would be the best way to get us off God's back? The teaching can hardly mean this. In other parables of Jesus there is usually the "How much more?" principle. This was a principle of interpretation adopted and in common use by the rabbis. It was known as the *Qal Wahomer*, the argument from light to heavy. Applying this rule to the parable of the friend at midnight in Luke's Gospel, we could have the following paraphrase: "If a neighbor will aid a person through his persistence, how much more will God answer those who continually cry out to him."

We are still left with the question about the necessity for perseverance in our prayers to God. Even before we pray, God knows our needs (Matt 6:8). Prayer is a means of establishing an agreement between the will of God and people's desires. Persistence tests our sincerity and the necessity for our requests. When we repeatedly ask God for something, our desires may become less intense. We begin to understand that our petitions are not in accord with the character of God revealed in Jesus Christ. Only through tireless efforts in telling God what we want do we fully comprehend what we need.

In Matthew 7:7 the author uses three injunctions that were given to the disciples. They are ask, seek, and knock. William Manson has suggested that these injunctions may mean asking for what we have never had, seeking those things which we lost, and knocking on doors of opportunities which have never been opened to us.[2] In verse nine, Jesus shows how asking applies to a family situation. If a son should ask his father for a loaf of bread, would the father be so heartless as to give his son a stone? Would he be so ruthless to give a stinging scorpion in place of a fish? What father could be so cruel? Jesus knew that the general tendency among people in motive and deed was to follow their evil impulses. Evil inclinations, however, do not prevent normal parents from giving good things to their children.

Jesus argued from the lesser to the greater and applied the principle of "How much more?' If a man who generally does that which is evil will give what is good to his children, how much more will God, who is loving, gracious, and merciful, give good things to those who ask of him. Luke has substituted Holy Spirit for "good things." Since there are few references in the Synoptic Gospels to the Holy Spirit and most of them are found in Luke's Gospel, Matthew's "good things" should be preferred to Luke's "Holy Spirit." Luke's interpretation reflects the coming of God's Spirit upon the early Christian community.

The character of God gives us direction in all our praying. When we make our petitions known to God, we do so on the assumption that we have some real knowledge about God's ways and thoughts. What we know of God comes to us through revelation in Jesus Christ. For this reason, we call upon God through the name of Jesus Christ. Christ's name stands for his character. Through his character, we know what God is like. Sometimes it is very frightening when we close our prayers in the name of Christ. What were our requests? Were they consistent with the character of God revealed in Christ or did they downgrade the character of God?

We should pray sincerely and persistently. Whatever our requests may be, they should come from a heart single in its devotion. We must really mean what we say. This experience with God must move us to participate in the purpose of God's rule by pursuing truth, goodness, mercy, love, and peace. We should pray wisely and not thoughtlessly or irreverently. Whatever our pleas may be, we ought to expect a reply from God on the basis of God's judgment, not ours.

The Golden Rule

Matthew 7:12

Luke's Gospel contains a saying of Jesus that is quite similar in wording to what is recorded in Matthew 7:12. It is found in his Sermon on the Plain (6:31) and immediately follows the instruction of Jesus on loving one's enemies. This differs considerably from the context in which the similar saying is found in Matthew. In Matthew the saying, "So whatever you wish that men would do to you, do so to them" has no connection with what precedes or with what follows. Some get around this disjointedness by contending that verse 12 is a summary statement of the Sermon on the Mount, and in fact is the conclusion, while the rest of the sermon is an epilogue. To me this verse gives no appearance at all of being a summary statement. In my opinion Luke has the saying in the original context.

For centuries this teaching has been called "The Golden Rule." Actually it is not a rule but a principle. Matthew and Luke present the principle in its positive form. In Judaism it was known in the negative form. In the book of Tobit from the Apocrypha, Tobit gives a farewell speech to his son Tobias who is about to embark on a trip to get money from Gabael in Rages of Media. Among other bits of advice, Tobit tells his son Tobias, "And what you hate do not do to anyone" (4:15). Rabbi Hillel, the Babylonian rabbi who came to Jerusalem and established a school of thought in the latter part of the first century B.C., taught the same thing. He said, "What you hate, do to no man" and added "This is the whole Torah, the rest is commentary" (*Babylonian Talmud Sabbat* 31a).

Christian commentators declare that the positive form is superior and more noble. On the other hand, many Jewish scholars argue for the superiority of the negative. This contention rests on prejudice from both sides. To me it is a waste of time to debate the superiority of the positive or the negative because the results are the same. The unbiased commentator would not give a dime for the difference.

Unless this principle is qualified by those who believe in God and submit to God's rule, it can be used by the community of the evil, wicked, and depraved individuals who expect reciprocal action from their peers (as many through the years have done). Of course, belief in God is subsumed in the Sermon on the Mount.

Submission to God's Rule

Matthew 7:13–27

Matthew closed Jesus' Sermon on the Mount with a series of reflections on the difficulties and tests of submission to God's rule. What is the connecting link or continuity of the material in Matthew 7:13–27? Some suggest that the coherence lies in a series of warnings to the disciples. There is a warning against the easy way (vv. 13–14). Jesus also cautioned his followers against being misled by others (vv. 15–20), self-deception (vv. 21–23), and building on a wrong foundation (vv. 24–27). In his account of the Sermon on the Plain, Luke omitted the warning against the easy way but included the other warnings (Luke 6:43–49), except that against false prophets (Matt 7:15).

A Contrast between the Two Ways

Matthew 7:13–14

The epilogue to the Sermon on the Mount begins with verse 13. Note that the epilogue contains three pairs of contrasts. They are the broad and narrow ways, the good and bad trees, and the wise and foolish builders. The teaching on two ways was familiar to the Jews from the Old Testament. This theme also is found in apocryphal literature, rabbinic discussions, and the Qumran writings. Possibly the earliest statement is in Deuteronomy 30:15, which says, "See, I have set before you this day life and good, death and evil." Jeremiah had a similar saying, "Behold, I set before you the way of life and the way of death" (21:8). By implication the substance of Psalm 1 is a discussion of the two ways.

While the doctrine of the two ways was not original with Jesus, he used this familiar teaching of the Old Testament and contemporary Judaism to challenge the people to follow the constricted path of his new way of life. Jesus combined the Jewish figure of the two ways with two gates—one narrow and the other wide.

In the Sermon on the Mount, Jesus began his teaching by describing the characteristics of those who submit to God's rule (5:3–16). He went on to point out the differences between the new way and the old order of Jewish practices (5:17–6:18). Then Jesus concluded the sermon by applying the new life under this rule to the problems that disturb people (6:19–7:12). Beginning at verse 13 Jesus challenged his hearers to accept God's rule and redirect their lives in accordance with God's purpose for humanity.

In Luke 13:24 the metaphor is a door rather than a gate: "Make every effort to enter through the narrow door, because many, I tell you, will try to enter and will not be able to." In answer to the question about only a few people being saved (Luke 13:23) Jesus presented one door opening into a house where many sought entrance. The picture in Matthew's Gospel is that of a traveler who comes to the crossroads. Each road has a gate. One is narrow and the other is wide. The narrow gate is an entrance to a hard and constricted way of life, but the wide gate leads into a road that is broad and easy. It is up to the traveler to make the choice of his or her direction.

The wide gate and the broad way require no effort, no self-discipline, no self-denial from the pilgrim. This way suggests more freedom and fewer restrictions. This way is easy to find because it is very popular. This way is the way of the multitudes. No effort is required in order to stay on this road because one is pushed along by the crowds. The broad and easy way is very inviting. The choice of the road should not be determined by how it looks initially but by where it takes us. The wide gate and the broad way lead to destruction. Why should one pay a high price for a fictitious happiness that proves to be destructive? Why should a person reject the true discipline that leads to genuine life?

Contrariwise, the way that leads to life is not easy to find. The gate is narrow and can be easily overlooked. The road is little trodden, so it could become hard and troublesome to travel. It is also a lonely road because there are not many companions.

We are not to suppose that the restrictions suggested by the narrow gate and difficult way are to be considered infringements of our rights or freedom. On the contrary, they imply protective measures against the evil forces of life. They are like the regimen an athlete follows in order to achieve goals. They promote a life of disciplined service where there is perfect freedom. Also we are not to conclude from the "few" and the "many" in this passage that only a small number of people will be saved by the preaching of the gospel. Jesus was describing the situation of his day. He was the leader of a small company of disciples who were the new remnant of God. Our concern is not to speculate about how many are saved but that we ourselves are right with God.

Beware of False Prophets

Matthew 7:15–20

In Matthew 7:15–20 Jesus cautioned his disciples concerning false prophets. Who were the false prophets Jesus had in mind? It is doubtful that he was speaking against the Pharisees and Sadducees, since neither group claimed the prophetic role in Judaism. It is true that the Pharisees claimed that they were the successors to the prophets, but they made it clear that they did not stand on the same level as the prophets. The false prophets, however, seem to have been the immoral, heretical, and unrecognized teachers in the Christian community. Since only Matthew, among the four evangelists, mentioned the false prophets, we assume that they were Christians who misinterpreted the demands of the gospel. They wanted to be Christians without accepting any ethical principles to guide them.

The hypocrisy of the spurious teachers is so complete in every way that it is hard to detect them. The teachers disguise themselves with sheep's clothing. Sheep's clothing is symbolic of their innocent appearance craftily assumed for the evil purpose of deceiving. Externally these teachers appear to be innocent sheep, but inwardly they are ferocious wolves. "Wolves" is a familiar Old Testament symbol for the enemies of God's flock (Ezek 22:7; Zeph 3:3). Matthew called the false prophets "ferocious" because they were greedy and ravaged the Christian community.

How can we distinguish between the false teacher and a true teacher? The laws of nature and fruit are just as applicable in the world of personality as they are in horticulture. Jesus laid down one criterion for making a judgment. By their fruits we shall recognize the difference between genuine and spurious prophets. Proverbs 20:11 says, "Even a child is known by his actions, by whether his conduct is pure and right." Jesus went on to say that it is equally impossible to obtain true teaching from false prophets as it is to get grapes from thorn bushes and figs from thistles. The *Didache* gives a lengthy list of criteria for distinguishing false and true prophets. The single test of Jesus is in marked contrast to the many tests suggested in the *Didache*.

The illustration of the good and worthless trees in version 17 appears in James 3:12 and seems to be an echo of Jesus' teaching from the Sermon on the Mount. Jesus used the expression more than once (Matt 12:33). Paul may have had the illustration in mind when he contrasted the works of the flesh and the fruit of the Spirit (Gal 5:16–24). Paul described the fruit of the Spirit in verses 22–23 as "Love, joy, peace, patience, kindness, goodness, faithfulness, gentleness, and self-control." Jesus' illustration by no means instructs us in the way character is formed, but the character, however it may be formed, displays itself in the fruit. Like produces like.

Jesus' statement in verse 16 is repeated in verse 20 to point out again that the single criterion for making a judgment concerning teachers who come to them is to examine the fruit of their labor. But we might ask, "What is the fruit of a false prophet?" We have common sense enough to know. If a person's teaching generates division, prejudice, harshness, and self-esteem, we have a right to question that one's validity. Any teaching not consistent with the character of God revealed in Jesus Christ is always suspect.

The Danger of Self-Deception

Matthew 7:21–23

In verses 15–20 Jesus cautioned against being misled by others. In verse 21 he exhorted his disciples to guard against misleading themselves. Self deception can ultimately prove to be the worst sort. A person may do good deeds in the name of Christ and yet be an unregenerated person. We can fool ourselves into thinking that we have helped people and glorified God when in reality we have done it all for self. Self-examination does not come very easily. We let ourselves get in the way. The revelation of self-deception will manifest itself in the future. Jesus referred to "that day" (v. 22), which means the day of judgment when we shall see ourselves as we really are.

The repetition of the title "Lord" presumably expressed earnestness and zeal. Jesus knew that many of his listeners would praise him but refuse to follow his example and live a Christian lifestyle. Some cover up their disobedience by displaying excessive zeal. Jesus knew that not all who professed to be his followers would submit to the rule of God. Only those who did would gain access to it.

Many interpret verse 21 to be Jesus' reaction to lip service, but verses 22–23 seem to suggest something else. Those who deluded themselves into thinking that they were following the teachings of Jesus would be shocked at the end of the age when they were rejected. They will expect praise, appealing to their gifts of prophecy, demon exorcism, and mighty works. Their rejection will be based on their failure to know Christ in continuing fellowship and obedience. Their deeds were done in the name of Jesus, but he would say to them, "I never knew you" (v. 23). Were the works of these people unacceptable? Why were they called evildoers? The tendency in certain of the early Christian churches was to emphasize the importance of outward gifts such as speaking in tongues, prophesying, healing, and other ecstatic actions (e.g. the Gentile church of Corinth). As a result they neglected the greatest of all spiritual gifts—the gift of love. The apostle Paul faced a situation like this in the church at Corinth and reminded them of the primacy of loving action(see 1 Cor 13:1–3).

The saying "Lord, Lord" (v. 22) is not condemned by Jesus, but the mere repetition of the title will not express true faith or secure full submission to God's rule. We can be orthodox in our confession of faith and do many works in the name of Christ, but our orthodoxy and outward expression, no matter how fervent, are worthless without inward love, loyalty, and devotion to Christ.

The Parable of the Two Builders

Matthew 7:24–27

The parable of the two builders in verses 24–27 joins the action in verse 23 and forms a concluding statement for the whole body of Jesus' teaching in the Sermon on the Mount. The same parable appears in Luke's conclusion to the same sermon (6:46–49). The parable presents us with two kinds of hearers. One hears and obeys, but another does not. The person who hears and obeys is wise. He is like a wise man who builds his house on a rock foundation. The metaphor of building is appropriate. The person who pitches his tent plans to reside in a place for a short period of time. Should danger arise, he can take down his tent and move. A permanent structure must have a good and solid foundation to protect it against the danger that will certainly arise. This kind of structure will not collapse when the floods come.

In the days of stress and crises, the house established on a rock foundation remains secure and firm. The storms and floods cannot move it. In like fashion the followers of Christ who hear and practice his teachings will have a sure foundation in the time of testing. Contrasted with the wise builder is the foolish man who built his house on shifting sand. The sand is "hearing without doing" the teachings of Jesus. People may hear the teachings of Jesus but fail to put them into practice. In the day of crisis, this sort of person will not be able to stand the test.

True religion is not easily distinguished from the counterfeit until it is put to the test. The real proof of genuineness is action. But if the goal of our doing is to satisfy our own pride and win praise from others, the moral and spiritual quality vanishes.

Right desire issues in right deed, but deeds without desire are worthless.

The Thrust of the Sermon

The Sermon on the Mount does not attempt to give all of the teachings of Jesus. Many other truths are given about God in the parable. In fact, some of the teachings of the sermon are clarified in the parables. The Sermon on the Mount should not be construed as a blueprint for an ideal society, as a theological creed, or as a code of ethics. Admittedly, the teachings have awakened people's consciences through the ages and stimulated them to make social, political, and religious reforms. In this sense the sermon performed the function of a mirror to reflect our sins. But the real thrust of the sermon is to confront people with the sovereignty of God and to call them to make a decision to submit to the will of God.

Many will ask, "Is it possible to fulfill all of the principles delineated by Jesus in the Sermon on the Mount?" Perhaps the real question to ask is, "Do I acknowledge the reality of God's will?" This is the "revolutionary challenge of the Sermon on the Mount, directed towards those who merely live by 'What has been said by men of old,' and who understand the will of God to be a protection and guarantee of sacred religious and moral tradition."[3]

Endnotes

1. H.D.A. Major, T.W. Manson, and C.J. Wright, *The Mission and the Message of Jesus* (London: Ivor Nicholson and Watson, Ltd., 1937), 466.

2. William Manson, "The Gospel of Luke," *Moffatt's New Testament Commentary* (London: Hodder and Stoughton 1945), 137.

3. Günther Bornkamm, *op. cit.*, 107.

Questions for Reflection

1. In Matthew 7:1–5 what kind of judgment is Jesus discussing?

2. After we clear our eyes of blind spots, are we then allowed to judge people?

3. Why should we persevere in our praying?

4. Is it possible for the Golden principle to be used by people with evil intentions?

5. Was the doctrine of two ways original with Jesus?

6. How are we to distinguish between false teachers and true teachers?

7. Is it possible for us to deceive ourselves?

8. How can we distinguish true religion from the spurious?

A SELECTED BIBLIOGRAPHY

Branscomb, B. H. *Jesus and the Law of Moses*. New York: Richard Smith, Inc., 1930.

Bornkamm, Günther. *Jesus of Nazareth*. Translated by Irene and Fraser McLusky with James Robinson. New York: Harper & Row, 1960.

Bultmann, Rudolf. *History of the Synoptic Tradition*. Translated by John Marsh. New York: Harper & Row, 1963.

________________. *Theology of the New Testament*. Volume 1. Translated by Kendrick Grobel. New York: Charles Scribner's Sons, 1951.

Daube, David. *The New Testament and Rabbinic Judaism*. London: The Athlone Press, 1956.

Davies, W. D. *The Setting of the Sermon on the Mount*. Cambridge: Cambridge University Press, 1964.

____________. *The Sermon on the Mount*. Cambridge: Cambridge University Press, 1969.

Dibelius, Martin. *The Sermon on the Mount*. Translated by C. H. Kraeling. New York: Charles Scribner's Sons, 1940.

Gaster, Theodor. *The Dead Sea Scriptures*. New York: Doubleday & Co., 1956.

Manson, William. *Jesus the Messiah*. Philadelphia: The Westminster Press, 1946.

________________. *The Gospel of Luke*. Moffatt's New Testament Commentary. London: Hodder & Stroughton, 1945.

Major, H. D. A., T. W. Manson, and C. J. Wright. *The Mission and Message of Jesus*. London: Ivor Nicholson & Watson, LTD., 1937.

McArthur, H. K. *Understanding the Sermon on the Mount*. New York: Harper & Row, 1960.

Montefiore, C. G. *The Synoptic Gospels*. Volume 2. London: Macmillan & Co., 1909.

________________. *Rabbinic Literature and Gospel Teachings*. London: Macmillan & Co., 1930.

Thurneysen, Eduard. *The Sermon on the Mount*. Translated by William and James Robinson. Richmond: John Knox Press, 1964.

Windisch, Hans. *The Meaning of the Sermon on the Mount*. Translated by S. M. Gilmour. Philadelphia: The Westminster Press, 1940.

SUGGESTIONS FOR STUDY

Dr. T. C. Smith's *Study Guide to the Sermon on the Mount* is designed to lead students of the Bible (and that includes all of us, from the beginner to the scholar) in an intensive exploration of the message and meaning of one of the greatest passages of Scripture. As one of Southern Baptists' foremost New Testament scholars, Dr. Smith presents here a challenging approach. Those who take up the challenge will discover new insight into this great sermon from Jesus.

The following suggestions for study are intended to aid those who use this book as a part of their investigation of the Sermon on the Mount (especially those engaged in an annual Bible study emphasis) so that they may maximize their efforts and receive the greatest benefit.

1. The Questions for Reflection at the end of the chapters can be used for personal study or group discussion. Study leaders may elect to ask study participants to research the answers to the Questions for Reflection ahead of the study sessions and to come prepared to give brief reports.

Churches may choose to acknowledge participation in this study by awarding a Study Certificate for those who prepare written answers to the Questions and attend each of the study sessions.

2. The book is designed primarily for a series of five, six, or seven study sessions extending over four days. Many churches have found the Sunday evening through Wednesday evening format to be ideal for such study. Of course, other formats are also possible, and churches may choose to extend their study through several weeks of Sunday evenings or Wednesday evenings.

A church may elect to follow this suggested schedule.

Sunday Evening:

Session One — The Introduction
Session Two — Chapter 1, The Beatitudes

Monday Evening:

Session Three — Chapter 2, The Six Contrasts: Parts One and Two
Session Four — Chapter 2, The Six Contrasts: Part Three

Tuesday Evening:

Session Five — Chapter 3, Worship: A More Excellent Way
Session Six — Chapter 4, Possessions and Anxiety

Wednesday Evening:

Session Seven — Chapter 5, Miscellaneous Teachings of the Sermon

3. The use of this book can be enhanced by reference to other books or articles on the Sermon on the Mount. In addition to the works listed in the Bibliography persons may consider consulting the works listed below in order to find valuable supplemental material. Each of these is available from

Smyth & Helwys Publishing, Inc.
P. O. Box 72
Greenville, South Carolina 29602
1-800-747-3016

Bauman, Clarence. *The Sermon on the Mount: The Modern Quest for Its Meaning.* Macon: Mercer University Press, 1985.

Those interested in how some of the most important biblical scholars and theologians of the modern period have understood the Sermon on the Mount will find the fullest account possible in this book.

Mills, Watson, *et al.* Editor. *Mercer Dictionary of the Bible.* Macon: Mercer University Press, 1990.

A project of the National Association of Baptist Professors of Religion, this award-winning volume contains hundreds of articles by Baptist professors and others. Many are most helpful to the study of the Sermon on the Mount. The range of subjects is broad and the information contained is extensive.

Nash, Scott. Editor and Contributor. *The Sermon on the Mount: Studies and Sermons*. Kerygma and Church Series. Greenville: Smyth & Helwys Publishing, Inc., 1992.

This volume in the Kerygma and Church series seeks to join the scholarly study of the text with its proclamation in the church. Several in-depth studies of sections of the Sermon by noted Baptists scholars, along with a number of insightful sermons by a broad spectrum of Baptist preachers, provide a solid basis for understanding the message of the Sermon and its implications for the life of the church.

Tilley, W. Clyde. *The Surpassing Righteousness: Evangelism and Ethics in the Sermon on the Mount*. Greenville: Smyth & Helwys Publishing, Inc, 1992.

Dr. Tilley's book is non-technical in its approach and is a comprehensive examination of Jesus' emphasis on evangelism and ethics in the Sermon. Supplemental reading from this book would provide much devotional insight and would enable readers to see how the message of the Sermon can be applied to many current issues confronting the Christian and the church.